World Book Myths & Legends Series

CHINESE MYTHS & LEGENDS

AS TOLD BY PHILIP ARDAGH

ILLUSTRATED BY MICHEAL FISHER

World Book, Inc.
a Scott Fetzer company
Chicago

MYTH OR LEGEND?

Long before people could read or write, stories were passed on by word of mouth. Every time they were told, they changed a little, with a new character added here and a twist to the plot there. From these ever-changing tales, myths and legends were born.

WHAT IS A MYTH?

In early times, people developed stories to explain local customs and natural phenomena, including how the world and humanity developed. These myths were considered sacred and true. Most include superhuman beings with special powers.

WHAT IS A LEGEND?

A legend is very much like a myth. The difference is that a legend is often based on an event that really happened or a person who really existed in relatively recent times.

WHO ARE THE CHINESE?

Today the Chinese make up more than one fifth of the world's population. More people speak Mandarin Chinese than any other language in the world. But there are many different nationalities and groups of Chinese people, with their own cultures and traditions.

ANCIENT PEOPLES

China has been inhabited since 500,000 B.C. But the first real Chinese state didn't appear until about 1650 B.C., more than a thousand years after civilization began in ancient Egypt. This state grew in the fertile valley of the Huang He (Yellow River).

AN ISOLATED COUNTRY

China is a vast country that covers about 3,700,000 sq mi (9,583,000 sq km). In the past it was almost completely cut off from the rest of the world. Chinese people were kept in, and "outsiders" were kept out by sea to the east and mountains and steppes to the north, south, and west.

THE SECRET OF SILK

Silk is made by silkworms that feed on mulberry leaves, then wrap themselves in a cocoon made of silk filament. By 2700 B.C. the Chinese had learned to spin thread from the cocoons to make silk and guarded the secret closely. Stories say that the secret of making silk spread to India in 140 B.C.

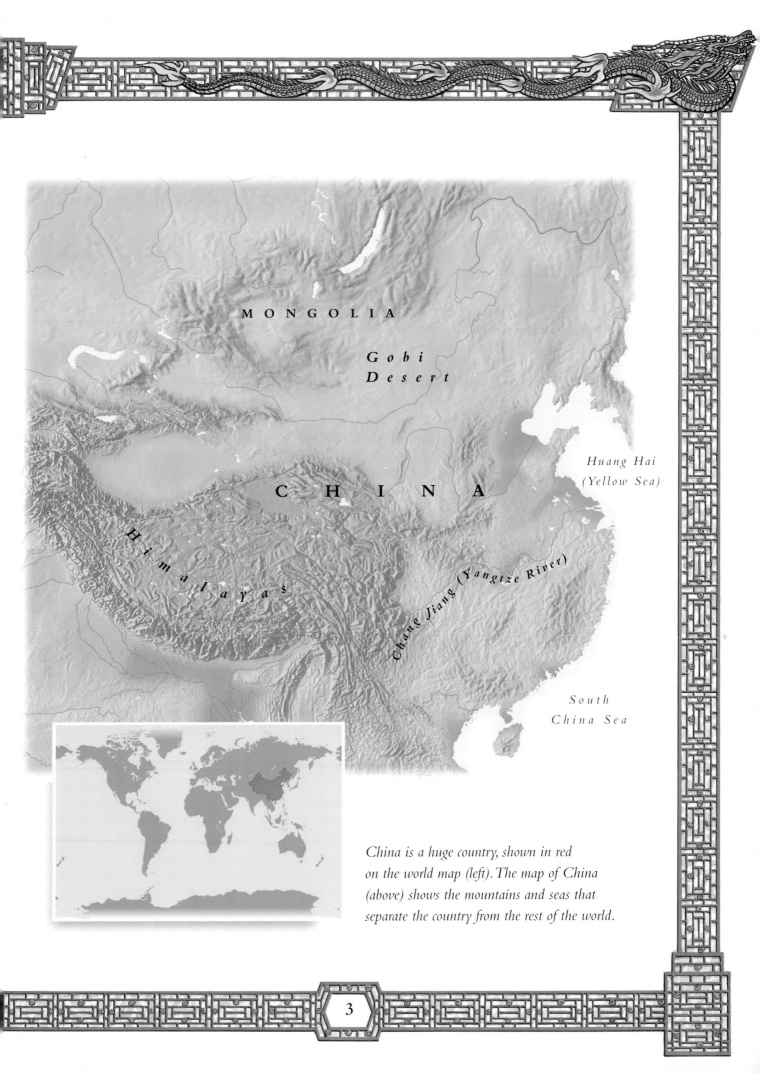

MONGOLIA

*Gobi
Desert*

CHINA

Himalayas

*Huang Hai
(Yellow Sea)*

Chang Jiang (Yangtze River)

*South
China Sea*

China is a huge country, shown in red
on the world map (left). The map of China
(above) shows the mountains and seas that
separate the country from the rest of the world.

TALES FROM CHINA

Chinese myths and legends are a blend of old beliefs
and the stories and beliefs of three main religions:
Confucianism, Taoism, and Buddhism.

COMMUNIST CHINA

Today China is a communist country. This
means that all land and property are owned by
the state rather than belonging to individuals.
Religion plays no part in communism, but it
is still important to many Chinese people.

OLD BELIEFS

The earliest Chinese religion included a belief
in life after death, the worship of ancestors,
and the belief that the first 12 emperors were
gods. A whole legendary period of history was
created, with a man called Yu as the first human
ruler. Historians and archaeologists are still
trying to find out how much of this legend
is based on truth.

CONFUCIANISM

Confucianism is more a way of life–a
philosophy–than religion. It is a belief that
places great importance on developing moral
character and responsibility. It is based on
the teachings of Confucius (551–479 B.C.),
also known as Kong Fu Zi. He taught ideas
of good government, and his followers
(called Confucians) became excellent
and powerful administrators.

THE WORKS OF CONFUCIUS

Temples were built to honor Confucius, and
some people tried to declare him a god.
Confucius is traditionally said to have written
many books, including the famous *Yi Jing* (*The
Book of Changes*). Unfortunately much of his
writing was destroyed in 213 B.C. on the orders
of the first emperor of all China, and no book
that was definitely written by Confucius exists.

TAOISM

Later thinkers developed the idea of "oneness"
of everything–that, if everything were somehow
connected, it must be possible to find a way to
live simply and in harmony with nature. Tao
was believed to be the way. (Tao and Taoism
are also written in Western spelling as Dao and
Daoism.) A book called *Tao Te Ching*, or *Dao
De Jing*, which means "the way and the power,"
is the center of Taoist beliefs. It is a collection
from several sources, and its authors and editors
are unknown.

BUDDHISM

Buddhism began in India but spread to China sometime in the first century A.D. It became one of China's three great religions. The founder of Buddhism was Buddha himself, probably born in the 500s or 400s B.C. He was originally named Siddhartha Gautama, and called Fo in Chinese. Buddha promised those who followed his strict laws and gave up worldly pleasures that they would leave the world of life and death and enter a blissful state called nirvana.

NOTE FROM THE AUTHOR

Myths and legends from different cultures are told in very different ways. The purpose of this book is to tell new versions of these old stories, not to copy the way in which they might have been traditionally told. The pictures that accompany the tales are not set in one particular period of history, but are intended to give a flavor of life in ancient China. I hope that you enjoy these stories and that this book will make you want to find out more about China, its peoples, its history, and its myths and legends.

This wooden carving is just one example of the fascinating styles of Chinese art. It shows one of the Eight Immortals, a group of ancient Chinese heroes.

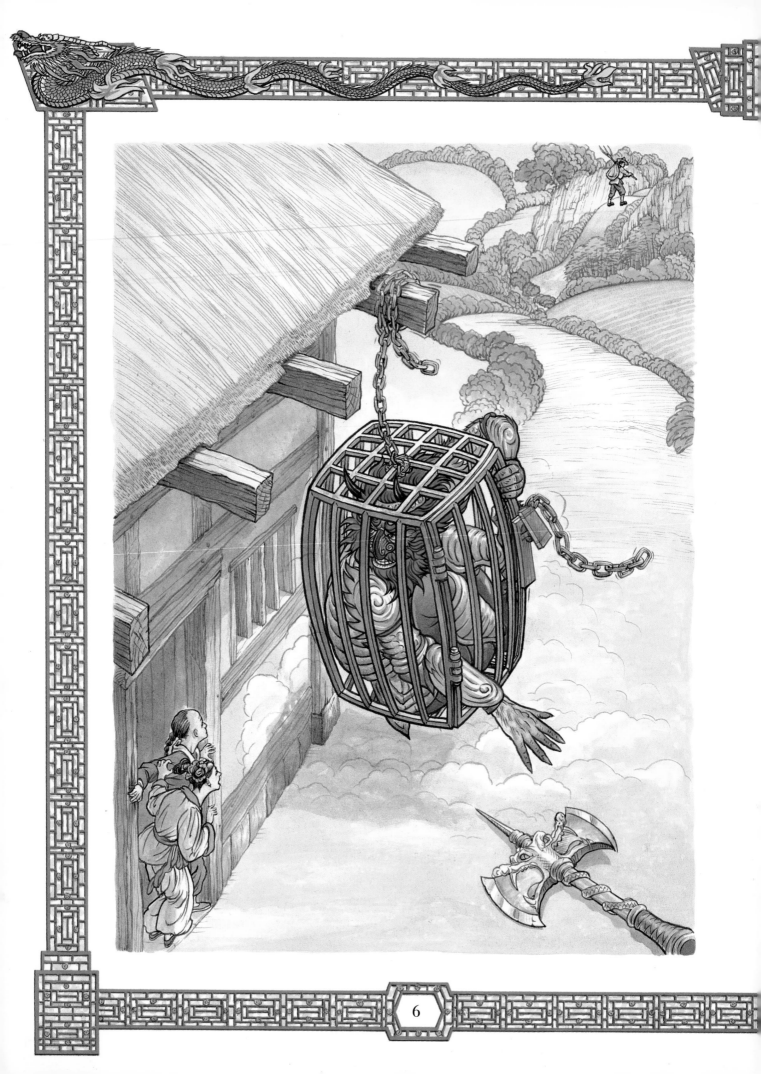

GOURD GIRL AND GOURD BOY

**This is the ancient myth of Nü Wa and Fu Xi.
It tells of the foolishness of their father, a rash
act of kindness, and the destruction of humankind.
It is also a tale of hope and new beginnings.**

One day a farmer was out in the fields when he heard a rumble of thunder.

"I've just about had enough of you, Thunder God!" he shouted. "I know you send down thunder and rain just to upset me." He cursed the god. "Come and get me!" he yelled. "I'm ready for you!"

The farmer hung a great big iron cage outside his house.

"Stay inside the house until I tell you to come out," he ordered his son and daughter. "There's some serious fighting to be done."

The Thunder God had heard the farmer's cursing and was angry with him, so—with a mighty crash of thunder and a brilliant flash of lightning—he appeared above the farmhouse.

"Come down here and face me, you coward!" yelled the angry farmer. "Don't stay up there in the clouds."

So the Thunder God came crashing down to Earth, clutching an enormous battle-ax. The farmer only had the iron fork he used in the field, but he also had the advantage. He was used to standing on the ground and on his own two feet, and he was ready and waiting for this god, who was shaking with rage.

With one swift movement the farmer caught him on the prongs of the fork. Before the god knew what was happening, he was flipped into the cage, and the door was slammed shut.

"There!" said the farmer triumphantly. "You can rumble and rage as much as you like now, but you can't bother me." Soon the rain stopped, and the clouds cleared. The god had been defeated.

Next morning the farmer decided to go to market to buy some herbs.

"I think I'm going to pickle the Thunder God for all to see," he told his son and daughter. "You must stay well clear of the cage and don't talk to the Thunder God, whatever he might say to try to frighten you," he insisted. "And most importantly of all," he added, with a stern face, "you must not give him a drink." With that he set off to market, feeling very proud of himself.

The farmer's son and daughter watched the god in the cage from a safe distance. He seemed harmless enough behind bars, looking sad and defeated.

As the day went on, the sun shone brightly, and the children became thirsty. They had a drink. The Thunder God watched a bead of water trickle down the girl's chin.

"Please let me have some water," he said. His voice was weak and whining, nothing like the loud bellowing of the day before. "Please."

"We're not allowed to talk to you," said the girl.

"And we're certainly not allowed to give you any water," said the boy.

"I'm sure your father didn't know today was going to be so hot," said the Thunder God. "On a day as hot as this, everyone should be allowed at least a sip of water–gods and humans alike."

"Our father forbade it," said the girl.

"For your own safety, I'd say," said the Thunder God, clutching the bars. "He was probably worried that I'd try to grab you if you gave me a drink."

"Exactly," said the boy.

"But what if I was to give you my word that I would not touch you?" said the Thunder God. "It is so hot, and I am so thirsty, locked away in this iron cage . . . . I am a god; I will not break an oath."

The farmer's daughter looked at the god, trapped in the iron cage in the brilliant sunshine. He was unable to move into the shade.

"Surely a few sips of water can't do any harm, can they?" she asked her brother.

"Not if he's given his word not to touch us," said the boy.

So the two children went expressly against their father's orders and gave the Thunder God a drink. Of course, what they didn't know—and their father had neglected to tell them—was that the Thunder God drew his strength and power from water. No sooner had a drop passed his lips than he swelled in size and broke free from the iron cage as though it were made of nothing more than rice paper.

The children shrank back in terror when they realized what they'd done.

"Don't be afraid," said the Thunder God. "I said I would not lay a finger on you. Here is something for your kindness," and he pulled a tooth from his mouth and threw it down before them. "From this day on, little sister, your name is Nü Wa and yours, little brother, is Fu Xi. Now plant the tooth and use the fruit it bears wisely," he said, and with that he was gone back to the heavens.

Nü Wa looked at her brother.

"What have we done?" she said. "What will Father say when he comes back and finds the Thunder God gone?"

"Perhaps if we plant the magic tooth, it will grow into something to please Father on his return," said Fu Xi.

They planted the tooth, and in next to no time, a tree sprang from the ground, bearing a single gourd that grew bigger and bigger and bigger.

"No wonder he called us Nü Wa and Fu Xi," said his sister, because the names mean Gourd Girl and Gourd Boy. "But what use is a huge gourd to us?" They watched in wonder as the gourd kept on growing.

Just then it started to rain again, and by the time their father had returned from the market with his pickling herbs, there were deep puddles around the farmhouse.

"You realize what you've done, don't you?" said their father.

"The Thunder God has gone back to Heaven and is going to flood Earth in revenge! Everyone will drown, thanks to you!"

This was a terrible thing to say, for it was the farmer who had captured the Thunder God and angered him in the first place, not the children. And still the waters rose.

"I'm going to have to build a boat for us," said their father. "I pronged the Thunder God with a fork of iron, I trapped him in a cage of iron, so I'll build a boat of iron." He set to work, and the children could hear the clanging of metal above the pouring of rain.

Soon the iron boat was finished, but his children would not climb aboard. Nü Wa and Fu Xi remembered what the Thunder God had said about his magic tooth when he gave it to them—*use the fruit it bears wisely*. Hadn't he named them Gourd Girl and Gourd Boy? Why was the giant gourd so important? Because they could hollow it out and use it as a boat of their own!

So, despite the protests from their father as he clambered into his own boat, the children stepped into the giant gourd . . . and the flood waters rose higher and higher and higher until the two vessels finally reached the gates of Heaven.

No human had reached the gates before, so when the farmer banged hard on them with his fists and called for help, the Lord of Heaven was startled.

"What is that dreadful noise?" he demanded.

The lesser Water God nervously explained. "The Thunder God was trapped by a human, so he asked me to flood Earth in revenge."

"Any higher, and your water will start to flood the heavens, too," said the Lord of Heaven angrily. "Make the waters go!"

"Y-Yes, Lord," said the Water God. He was so quick to please his master that he made the flood subside far too fast. One second there was water holding up the iron boat and the gourd, and the next moment there was none.

Both the iron boat and the gourd came hurtling back down to Earth at a terrible speed. The iron boat landed with a mighty crash, killing the farmer in an instant. Luckily for Gourd Girl, Nü Wa, and Gourd Boy, Fu Xi, they had a soft landing. Their giant gourd hit the ground and bounced a few times; then the pair tumbled out onto the damp soil with nothing more than a few bruises. They were the only two people left alive on the entire Earth.

When they became adults, Nü Wa gave birth to a ball of flesh. She and Fu Xi carried it up a ladder lowered from Heaven and cut the ball into small pieces. These they scattered in the wind, and each piece that landed on Earth became a human being. Nü Wa and Fu Xi became gods.

The Archer and the Suns

According to some of the earliest Chinese myths, every living thing is part of the oneness of the universe and is made up of three things: the yin, the yang, and the gi. They are held by the yin, carried by the yang, and kept together by the energy of gi.

Yin is female. She is the moon. She is water. She is the cold. She is autumn and winter. She is the shadows.

Ying is male. He is the sun. He is dry land. He is the heat. He is spring and summer. He is the brightness.

Yin fights yang. Yang fights yin. They are locked in an evenly matched fight to take control. The fight goes on, and the natural balance is maintained. Sometimes the balance is tipped, and it takes a hero to put things right. Yi the archer was such a hero.

Beyond the horizon of the Eastern Sea, in a hot spring, there was a giant mulberry tree that reached the skies. It was called Fu Sang and was home to the ten sons of Di Jun–God of the Eastern Sky–and his goddess bride, Xi He. Their children were suns, and they took turns walking across the sky, bringing warmth and life to Earth below. Each morning, it was the turn of one sun to make his journey. While he made his way across the sky, the other nine had to remain in the branches of Fu Sang.

Xi He ruled that there must never be more than one of her sons in the sky at any one time. And that's the way it was for a thousand years.

But the suns grew tired of the same routine, day in and day out. They wanted to do something different.

"The only time we can play together is here in the tree," said one.

"Wouldn't it be fun to chase each other across the sky!" said another.

"Why don't we?" suggested a third.

"We can't," said a fourth.

"Why not?" demanded a fifth.

"Because our mother forbids it," said a sixth.

"But why does she forbid it?" wondered a seventh.

"I'm sure the humans would be pleased," protested an eighth.

"We bring them warmth and light and help their crops grow," agreed a ninth.

"So let's all go out together tomorrow morning!" said the tenth, for it was nighttime, and they were all together on the branches of Fu Sang.

The next morning, before Xi He arrived in her chariot, all ten suns jumped out of the tree and chased one another across the sky, laughing and playing.

Down below on Earth the people were delighted.

"What a beautiful day!" they cried. "What a glorious sight! How lucky we are to have ten suns, not just one."

But it wasn't long before the delight turned to horror and fear. Ten times the number of suns meant ten times the brightness and ten times the heat. Crops shriveled and died and were burned to a crisp. People were blinded by the brightness. Lakes and rivers dried up, and rocks began to melt in the terrible heat. Wild animals came out of the dead, dry forests in search of food and water, and attacked people. Terrifying beasts awoke from sleep and plagued the land. The situation became desperate . . . but still the ten brother suns played up in the sky.

Di Jun and Xi He saw the harm their children were causing the people and pleaded with them to return to the mighty mulberry tree. They refused. The suns had tasted freedom, and they loved it!

A man called Emperor Yao prayed to the god and goddess for help. Emperor Yao was no ordinary emperor. He did not live in a palace with hundreds of servants, feast on exotic foods, or wear fine silks. He preferred to live among his subjects. His home was a simple peasant's shack, his clothes were ordinary, and he ate porridge made from local wild grains. He was a humble man and a good leader, so Di Jun decided to help him.

The god sent Yi the Archer to Emperor Yao with ten magical arrows in his quiver—one for each sun. Emperor Yao was delighted by Yi's arrival. The archer brought his wife, Heng E (also called Chang E), with him, and the emperor made them both welcome.

Yi took up his bow, notched the first magical arrow, took aim, and fired it at the center of one of the suns. There was an enormous explosion, sparks flew, and the sun disappeared. Something hurtled to the ground and landed nearby. Those people brave enough to venture out of doors in the heat hurried to the spot where the object had fallen. It was a three-legged raven with Yi's arrow through its heart. This was the spirit of the sun.

Yi notched a second arrow, then a third, then a fourth. Each time he extinguished a sun, a three-legged raven fell to earth, the sky became a little bit less bright, and the temperature dropped. Faster and faster, Yi destroyed the rebel suns.

Emperor Yao eyed Yi's quiver. There had been ten arrows in it, but now that the archer had destroyed eight suns, only two remained. Two arrows for two suns. What if Yi the Archer used both the arrows? There would be no suns left. No daylight. No warmth. No energy to grow his people's crops.

Emperor Yao slipped an arrow from the quiver, so when the spirit of the ninth sun fell to the ground as a raven, Yi found that he had run out of arrows and his job was done. One sun remained in the sky, which is just as it should be.

"On behalf of all my people, I thank you," said Emperor Yao, and he also gave thanks to Di Jun and Xi He.

But Di Jun, God of the East and Lord of Heaven, was less pleased with Yi.

"You did as I asked, Yi," he said. "I do not deny that. But I cannot bear to face you every day in Heaven. Every time I see you, I'll be reminded of my dead children. You and your wife, Heng E, must leave Heaven forever."

Heng E thought that it was most unfair to be banished to live among humans. After all it had been her husband who had fired those arrows, not she. She noticed a change come over him. It was obvious that he was now keeping secrets and hiding things from her.

Yi had been to Mount Kunlun to visit the Queen Mother of the West. In just 16 days he had built her the most splendid palace on Earth, with walls of the smoothest polished jade, sweet-scented timbers, and a roof of glass. What Heng E didn't know was that her husband had been given a Pill of Immortality in return–one of the pills that helped the gods to live forever.

The Queen Mother of the West, a goddess, had instructed Yi the Archer carefully about the use of this pill. It should be shared–it was too powerful for one person alone–and should be eaten only after one's body had been properly prepared for it. On his return Yi hid the pill, wrapped in a piece of silk, in the rafters of their home.

One day when Yi was away, Heng E was puzzled by a strange, magical glow coming from the rafters. She climbed up onto a beam and discovered the Pill of Immortality. Its magic was so strong that its power shone through the cloth.

She was just touching the pill with the tip of her tongue to taste it when Yi strode into the house. Some claim that Heng E then deliberately swallowed the pill. Others say she was so surprised by her husband's unexpected return that she swallowed it by mistake.

Either way, the pill—meant to be taken by two after careful planning—had now been swallowed by Heng E with no preparation at all!

The result was immediate. Heng E floated up off the rafter and out of the open door of their house, and there was nothing either of them could do about it. She had no control over her body.

Up she floated—up, up, up—until she reached the moon. There she landed, and there she is still, with a hare for company. The hare is forever pounding minerals and herbs with a huge pestle and mortar.

Yi, meanwhile, built himself a palace on the one remaining sun so that he could be up in the sky near his beloved wife. On the nights when the moon shines brightest, he is visiting her.

So Heng E, the moon goddess, gives the moon its yin—its female side, its coldness, its calm. Yi gives the sun its yang—its male side, its heat and fire. Together they balance day and night.

THE PRINCESS
AND THE HOUND

Each Chinese year is dedicated to one of 12
animals, ranging from the monkey to the rat.
This tale, based on an ancient Confucian myth,
tells how the Year of the Dog got its name.

There was once a young man called Wu, who was in love with a princess. He just couldn't help it. She was so beautiful that he couldn't take his eyes off her. Luckily for Wu, the princess felt the same about him. Unluckily for Wu, he was a lowly courtier, and there was no way that the princess's father, the emperor, would let them marry—so their love had to be secret.

One day the emperor caught Wu looking at his daughter with love and longing in his eyes, and the old man flew into a rage.

"How dare you look upon the princess in such a manner!" he bellowed. "You will leave this palace never to return! Be grateful I don't chop off your head."

The princess wanted to say something in Wu's defense—to tell her emperor father of their love—but she knew that this would probably make matters worse and decided to remain silent.

So Wu left the emperor's court with a heavy heart and, with no money or possessions, went to live in the mountains. He lived a disgraced life, and soon other misfits and outcasts, who had heard his sad story, came to live alongside him.

They became bandits, with Wu as their leader. With no land to grow rice and no money to buy it, a life of crime seemed the only answer. Wu's raiders became the terror of the foothills.

They raided farms and villages and robbed travelers on the roads.

It didn't take long for news of this to reach the emperor, and he ordered his army to stamp out the trouble. But Wu and his bandits knew the mountains better than anyone and disappeared behind outcrops, down gullies, or into caves hidden from view with branches.

Stories soon spread that Wu and his men could turn to mist and drift away on the wind at the first sign of trouble. This angered the emperor even more.

"Let it be known that whoever brings me the head of Wu will not only be awarded lands containing ten thousand families, but also the hand of my beautiful daughter, the princess, in marriage," he declared to the captain of the guard.

The proclamation soon spread around the kingdom. Meanwhile, the princess stayed in her room, refusing to eat and drink for three days and talking to no one. She became sickly and pale.

"What is wrong, Daughter?" asked her father at her bedside. Of course, he did not know of his daughter's love for the man he wanted dead.

She said nothing. There was a faraway look in her beautiful eyes.

A week later the emperor was sitting in a pagoda, the princess at his feet, when a servant hurried to them with incredible news.

"Lord and master," he said. "Come quickly to the palace gates for there is something you will be pleased to see."

Intrigued, the emperor strode through the garden to the courtyard, his daughter hurrying a few paces behind him. There, standing in the open gateway, stood a huge dog, with fur all the colors of the rainbow.

The emperor's jaw dropped open in amazement, and he was filled with happiness. It wasn't the dog's colors that pleased him, nor its enormous teeth and lolling tongue. No, what made the emperor happy was what was caught up in the matted hair hanging beneath the beast's slavering jaws—the severed head of Wu.

The emperor ordered Wu's head to be hung from the highest flagpole in the palace as a warning to those who dared look upon his daughter or lead raids against his people.

"Bring this honored dog the tastiest of morsels," the emperor ordered. "Have it bathed and its coat brushed until its rainbow colors gleam in their most radiant light . . . ."

"What are you doing, Father?" asked the princess.

"Why, I am rewarding the beast for a job well done," he said.

"But didn't you proclaim that whoever brought you the head of Wu should have lands containing ten thousand families?"

"Yes," agreed the emperor, "but what use are lands to this great beast?"

"You cannot go back on your word now, Father," said his daughter.

"You are right, of course," nodded the emperor. He cleared his throat and made an announcement to all those present in the palace.

"As proclaimed, I now reward this dog for bringing me the head of Wu by bestowing upon it lands containing ten thousand families."

There were gasps and mutterings of surprise from the courtiers.

"Aren't you forgetting something?" the princess whispered in the old man's ear. "You must marry me off to this slavering beast."

"No!" cried the emperor.

"Yes," said the princess. "What good is the emperor if he breaks his word?"

"Very well," said the emperor at last. "But it will be a wedding in name only, Daughter. I do not expect you to have to live with this creature as its wife."

So the day of the wedding came. The princess was dressed in her finest clothes, and the vows were announced. At the end of the ceremony, the dog, whom the princess had named Ban Hu, gently picked her up between its teeth and tossed her onto its back. Before anyone realized what was happening, or had time to do anything about it, the dog ran from the palace with the princess holding on to its fur for dear life.

"Stop them!" cried the emperor. "Stop them! If that treacherous beast harms so much as a single hair on my daughter's head . . . ."

As his lord and master raged, the captain of the guard gathered together his men, and they streamed out of the palace in pursuit of the enormous dog, the head of Wu still grinning from the flagpole high above them.

Soon the sky darkened, and there was a mighty storm, with thunder, lightning, and rain so heavy that each drop was like a blow to a man's back. The huge dog's paw prints were washed away, and the guards returned empty-handed.

"She is gone!" the emperor wailed. "Eaten, no doubt, by that multi-colored hound." And then he proclaimed that there would be 12 months of official mourning, when all those in the empire would grieve at the loss of his only daughter. "It shall be called the Year of the Dog," he declared.

The years passed, and the emperor lay dying, when in walked his beloved daughter, the princess. Looking up from his deathbed, he wept for joy.

"I thought you were dead," he said.

"No," said the princess. "I have lived the years with Ban Hu, across the mountains. He is dead now, but we had 12 children who have a present for their grandfather." She produced some sticks of licorice and put one in his mouth.

The emperor chewed on the stick, and the effect was magical. The years fell from him, and he was young again. He threw his arms around his daughter.

"Tell me about your husband," he pleaded.

"Very well," smiled the princess. "You see, Father, the hound and Wu were one and the same," she said. "I have always loved Wu. When you put out a reward for his head, I sent my spirit body to the mountains to find him."

"That was why you were so pale, with that faraway look in your eyes!" cried the emperor with sudden understanding. "Your spirit was off on a long journey!"

"Yes," said the princess. "And I found my beloved Wu where, with the help of my spirit body, he took on the form of the ancient dog god, Ban Hu. . . . The rest you know."

"But was he always in the form of a dog?" gasped the emperor.

"No," said the princess. "Sometimes he became the headless Wu."

"But that is terrible!" said the emperor.

"No," said the princess. "I loved him however he looked. Together we found nothing but happiness."

"And that is what you bring me, Daughter," said the emperor. "I misjudged Wu, and I am sorry. Welcome home."

And that is the tale of the emperor, the princess, and Wu, the lowly courtier, who fairly won her hand in marriage at a great price—that of his own head.

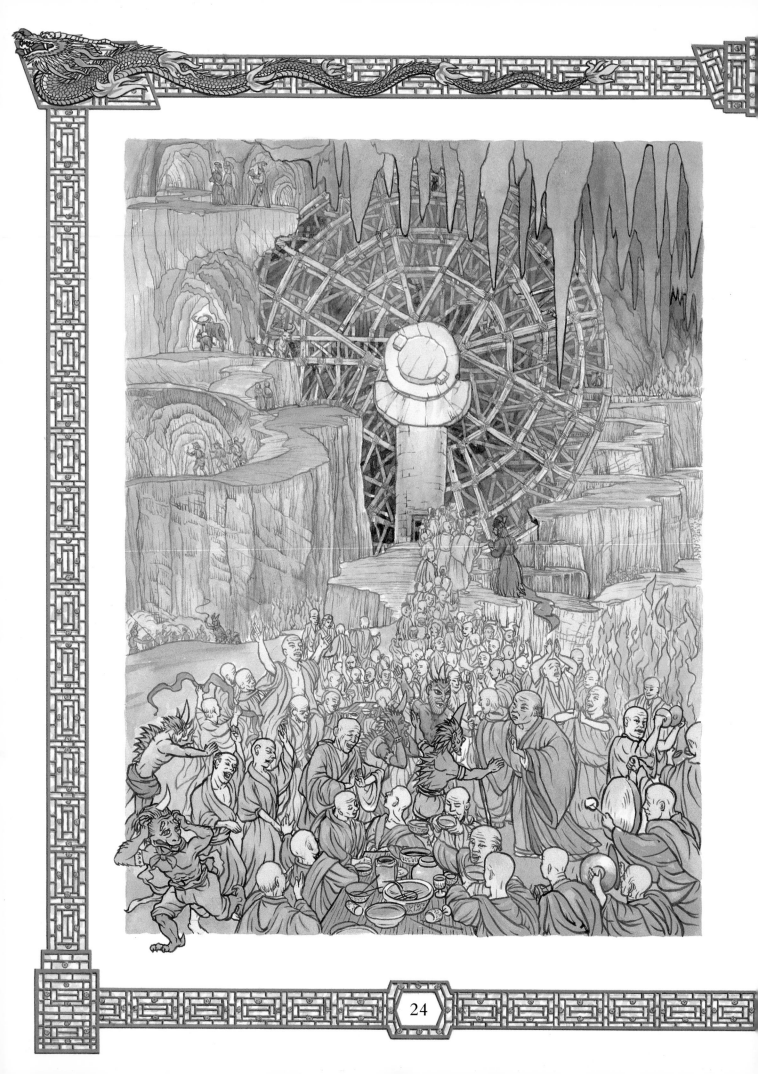

Journey into the Underworld

There is an ancient Chinese belief that after death a person's soul is judged and then placed in a new body. The identity of the new body depends on what the person has done in the past. Sometimes not everything goes as expected.

There was once a Buddhist monk who would not lie in bed at night and close his eyes. While other men and women slept, he sat bolt upright in a coffin, wide awake.

This monk did not seem to need sleep, and others soon spotted that there was something special about him.

"He must truly know the ways of enlightenment," said one.

"The gods must have great plans for him," agreed another.

When, years later, the monk died, he was laid out in the coffin he'd spent his nights in. He looked very peaceful and as though he were enjoying sleep for the first time.

People came to see the body of this strange holy man, and it soon became obvious that there was something unusual about his body, too. When ordinary people die, their bodies begin to decay, so their souls go down to the Underworld for judgment without them. This monk's body did not decay, and when he went to the Underworld, he took his body with him.

The Chinese Underworld was a series of courts where the souls of the dead were judged, punishments given out, and their next lives determined. When a soul reached the Underworld, it was taken to a court where it was weighed.

If the soul was heavy–weighed down with guilt at all the bad things it had done in life–it was passed onto another court to be judged.

Which court this was depended on the sins and crimes committed by the soul. There were different courts for different types of crimes, including greed, murder, lying, even failing to honor one's mother and father. The Buddhist monk did not visit these courts, but walked straight past them.

There was a wide range of different punishments, too. Some souls were thrown to wild beasts, some were nailed to beds, some were tossed into the flames. Each court sent its victims to a different awful place. The monk was careful to avoid these, too.

When the punishment was at an end, the souls reached the tenth and final court. This was where the decision was made on the new life a soul would have when passing to the Wheel of Transmigration. It was a matter of fitting old souls into new bodies, and choosing bodies that the souls deserved.

Good souls, which had been weighed and found light enough in the first court of the Underworld, passed straight to the Wheel of Transmigration. They were reincarnated as aristocrats. Souls who had been less good were sent back to Earth in the bodies of beggars or animals–but would always have a chance to better themselves the next time they died and were reborn.

As the monk stood watching the souls depart in their new bodies, one called to him as she passed through the gates of the Underworld.

"I remember you!" she called. "You mother's soul is still in terrible torment."

The monk was horrified. All the while he'd imagined his mother had been born again and was living happily on Earth in some new body. . . . Now he'd found out that her soul was still down there, somewhere, being tortured.

He hurried to the gates to find out more from the soul before she left. Just outside the gates stood the Lady Meng. She was handing each departing soul a cup of the Potion of Forgetting, called Mi Hun Tang. Once they had drunk the potion, the souls would remember nothing.

This was why no one could remember the Underworld or his or her previous lives. What the souls did remember, though, was the pain. Without the memory of pain, punishment would have been pointless.

The monk was too late. The soul who had called out to him had already drunk from the cup. She remembered nothing. There was no point in asking her where she had seen his mother's tortured soul.

Like the Chinese government in the upper world of Earth, and the gods above them in Heaven, the Underworld was run by many officials. Every department of each court had hordes of them. Some recorded the weight of the souls, some recorded the sins committed, some recorded the punishments given, some recorded when the sentences were at an end, and so on and so on.

All the monk knew was that his mother had always been very good as far as he was concerned. She'd been kind to everyone. He couldn't imagine that anything she had done was very bad, and he wanted to plead for her release. The only problem was, to whom should he plead? Which court? Which official? No one seemed interested, and soon his pleas turned to demands.

Because he still had his body, the dead monk could be much more of a nuisance than an ordinary soul awaiting judgment. He could go from place to place, trying to find out more information about his mother and demanding that she be set free.

Time after time he was met with the same official reply.

"The punishments that souls receive are for their past sins. Such punishments are drafted in Heaven and carried out in the Underworld. No one has the power to stop them."

"My mother will be the exception!" the monk insisted. He wasn't about to give up. He went from court to court, slamming doors behind him and making as much noise as possible.

"If they're going to be difficult about this, *I'm* going to be difficult!" he declared.

He visited each of the many jailers, demanding to know if his mother's soul was being punished there. Some jailers would turn him away. Others were more helpful, feeling sorry for the monk, and they would call out his mother's name above the wails of torment and despair. Still he couldn't find her.

The search went on. His mother had looked after him in life, so it seemed only right that he should try to help her soul in death . . . if he could find her. It wasn't long before just about every official in all the courts and every jailer knew the monk and dreaded his visits.

In desperation he decided to hold a banquet for the souls of all the other dead monks in the Underworld, while they were waiting to be given their new bodies and to pass onto the Wheel of Transmigration.

Many of them had known this devoted Buddhist monk in life– the monk who never slept, but sat upright in a coffin–and many had heard of his search for his mother's soul in the Underworld. They came in great numbers and made a great deal of noise.

It was chaos! The Underworld had never heard . . . never *seen* anything like it. The officials needed order to do their jobs. They needed peace and quiet, and that was something they'd had little of since the monk had begun searching for his mother's soul.

Enough was enough. The monk had won! The officials agreed to release his mother's soul sooner than planned, even if it was only in the body of a dog. At least it would get her back in the upper world and stop this soul–still with a body–from making such a fuss.

Some say that it was the Buddha himself who freed the woman's soul from the Underworld because he was so impressed by the monk's devotion to her. Whatever the reason, the monk had succeeded.

"Now, what about me?" said the monk. "In life I needed no sleep. In death my body has not decayed. Here in the Underworld you have done my bidding. What do you have planned for me?"

He felt sure that he would go to the tenth court and the Wheel of Transmigration and return to Earth as a higher being. He was wrong.

The gods had decided that, because he seemed so at home among the dead souls, he should stay there with them. They named him Di Zang Wang, which means King of the Earth's Womb, and made him Lord of the Underworld. The many awful places he had been so desperate to save his mother from were now part of his kingdom. Suddenly his years of sitting in the coffin made sense. We may not always get what we expect, but we are usually given what we deserve.

The newly named Di Zang Wang was given assistants to help him in his task. They included the powerful and impressive Yan Wang, God of the Dead and judge of the first court of the Underworld, and two extraordinary demon jailers—one with the head of an ox, the other with the head of a horse.

THE RICE ROAD

This Taoist myth shows the great gulf between the rich and the poor and how an honest magistrate was helped by one of the Eight Immortals to humble a greedy man.

The merchant and farmer Kuang Zi Lian was rich–very rich–and he loved to show off his wealth by having the biggest and best of everything. He owned thousands of fields, his clothes were made of the most exquisite and expensive silks, and his enormous home was crammed full of priceless treasures.

For his birthday he planned the most spectacular banquet that his neighbors had ever seen, and preparations were well underway. The dirt road to his home was bumpy and full of stones, so Kuang Zi Lian ordered a team of servants to clear them from the road. This was back breaking work, and the servants carried the stones away by the basketload.

When this was done, Kuang Zi Lian went to inspect the work and found that the road was now pitted with potholes where the stones had been.

"Have the holes filled and a red carpet laid on top, leading under the gatehouse, through my gardens, and up to the front door," he ordered.

"What shall they fill the holes with?" asked his secretary.

"Rice!" said Kuang Zi Lian, his face breaking into a smile. "And don't just fill the holes. I want a thick layer of rice under the carpet so that it's the smoothest of all walks for my guests!"

Now in China at that time, the poor ate nothing but rice, and the very poor were lucky to eat even that. To use this food in such a way was a terrible waste, but Kuang Zi Lian saw this as another way to show just how rich and important he was. Anyone could *eat* rice. Only he was rich and powerful enough to make a road out of it.

News of this waste–at a time when people were starving–reached the magistrate in the nearby town. His name was Zhao Shen Xiao, and he was a good and honest man, but there was nothing he could do about the rice road. Kuang Zi Lian could use his riches as he pleased. But Zhao Shen Xiao was saddened and thought of all the hungry people in the towns and villages.

News of Kuang Zi Lian's forthcoming banquet had reached the local beggars, and they made their way to his gatehouse with their begging bowls. They knew that there was rice beneath the carpet, but they did not dare take any for they knew it was not theirs to take.

They dared not step through the gatehouse and into the gardens either because they were under the watchful eye of the private guards. These guards had been given strict instructions by Kuang Zi Lian on how to treat unwanted visitors–and that was to treat them badly.

On the day of the banquet itself, however, one beggar could be found within the house. He walked among the armies of servants who were rushing here and there, finishing off the last-minute preparations. Delicious smells wafted from the kitchen, porcelain bowls glistened on row upon row of finely lacquered tables, statues were given a last-minute polish, and the carpet on the rice road was given a final dusting.

The beggar walked into the kitchen and held out his bowl.

"Could you spare any leftovers?" he begged. "My wife and children have not eaten for days."

But the cooks did not dare give him any food, in case news of it reached Kuang Zi Lian.

At that moment two guards entered and caught the beggar.

One wrenched the empty begging bowl from his hands, while the other grabbed him by the scruff of the neck and threw him down the outside steps to the ground. The beggar managed to lift a handful of rice from under the carpet before getting to his feet. His nose was bleeding from the fall.

The first guard grabbed his wrist and tightened his grip. "Put that back," he ordered.

The beggar let the rice trickle from his fingers. "How can your master miss a handful of rice for my starving children when he has a whole road of it?" he pleaded.

"Do not question us!" said the second guard, and following their master's instructions, they kicked him to the ground as a lesson to all the other beggars.

Then came the banquet. All the wealthy landowners arrived along the rice road, marveling at a host so fabulously rich that he could choose to use rice in this way. They admired Kuang Zi Lian's magnificent gardens, house, and treasures, and then all sat down for the splendid feast.

What began as cries of delight from the wealthy guests soon turned to shrieks of horror—for what had been bowls of rice turned to bowls of maggots, and noodles became writhing worms. Then the bowls themselves became too hot to hold, and the hands of the guests blistered in the painful heat. Even the finest rice wine took on the taste of mud water.

The guests were horrified, but none were more horrified than the host.

"There is trickery at work here!" he screamed, leaping to his feet. "Two of my guards reported trouble from a strange beggar. He must have cast a spell upon us. Rest assured that he shall be punished!"

The furious Kuang Zi Lian left the banquet and ordered his guards to take him to the beggar, who still lay bleeding on the ground.

A group of other beggars had crept into the gardens to try to help him.

"This is your doing!" raged Kuang Zi Lian, and he kicked the poor beggar, who took one last gasp of air then died.

Some of the beggars plucked up enough courage to report the murder to the magistrate Zhao Shen Xiao. He was outraged and made his way at once along the rice road, with a police escort, to Kuang Zi Lian's house.

When he arrived, he was surprised to see that the body of the beggar was still lying there. He'd expected that Kuang Zi Lian would have ordered it to be hidden in case there was an investigation. He soon discovered why it hadn't been moved. None of the servants could lift the dead man. His body was impossibly heavy.

Zhao Shen Xiao bent down and went through the pockets of the beggar, finding a single piece of paper. He unfolded the paper, read the few words upon it, then folded it again.

"Bring me Kuang Zi Lian," he ordered his escort.

Soon one of the richest men in the province stood before him.

"You killed this man," said Zhao Shen Xiao. "I have witnesses."

"He was a thief and on my property," sneered Kuang Zi Lian.

"Wrong," said the magistrate. "This was no thief or beggar. This was Li Xuan."

There were gasps of horror and surprise from the onlookers. Li Xuan (sometimes called Tie Guai Li) was one of the Eight Immortals– one of eight ordinary human beings who had found the road to truth and enlightenment through good deeds. This man in beggar's clothes who lay dead on the ground before them was almost a god.

Kuang Zi Lian threw himself to the ground and at the mercy of the magistrate.

"I didn't know . . . I didn't know . . . ," he wailed pathetically.

"Of course you didn't know," said Zhao Shen Xiao. "He came here to give you a test–a test that you failed. It cost Li Xuan his life.

What is to stop me from taking your life in return?"

"Spare me!" sobbed Kuang Zi Lian. "I will give away everything. Everything, starting with the rice road. Let the food be distributed to the poor. Let my riches be sold and the money be given to charity."

"Fine words," said Zhao Shen Xiao. "If you do this, I will spare you your life, so long as you spend the rest of it as a road sweeper."

"Anything!" cried Kuang Zi Lian. "Thank you."

Zhao Shen Xiao smiled to himself, remembering the piece of paper inside Li Xuan's pocket. It had said: "Spare Kuang Zi Lian's life. Make him a road sweeper." This was followed by his signature. There had been no demand that Kuang Zi Lian give away his riches. He had done that of his own free will.

When the beggars came to lift Li Xuan, he was as light as a feather. And soon after they placed him in a coffin, he disappeared. It takes more than that to kill one of the Eight Immortals. Li Xuan was back with the other seven, telling them the lessons he had taught that day.

THE UGLY ONE

Many people thought Kui (sometimes called Zhong Kui) was very ugly. But Kui not only was a great scholar, he also became a god. Statues to Kui stood in many homes, and most of them showed him standing on a giant turtle.

There are a number of different stories about why Kui was shown on a turtle. One of these tells how he came from a very poor family and how his parents sacrificed a great deal to help him with his studies. Neither of them could read or write, but they wanted the very best for their son. His success would bring honor to all the family.

"One day you might even become a government official," said his mother, little realizing that he would reach far greater heights than this.

From an early age Kui would study until it was too dark to read and then be up at first light, ready to start a new day of study. He had a thirst for knowledge.

He took local exams, then city exams, passing every one, all the way up to the provincial exams. He did well in every exam he took, but he was never boastful and always wanted to do better. Finally he was ready for the most important exams of all: the Imperial Examinations.

There was some stiff competition from the other candidates, but Kui had been working toward these exams all his life, so he hoped that he would have a good chance in them.

Although Kui hoped and prayed that he would do well, and he had worked so hard to do his very best, no one was more surprised than he was when he came out with top marks. He had entered the exams with some clever scholars, and he had done better than all of them.

"Because you came first, it is a tradition that the emperor himself will give you your honors at the palace," the examiners told him.

Kui's family was very proud of him. His mother and father had traveled to the Imperial City to be near him on this important day.

"No one could ask for a better son," said Kui's mother, giving him a warm embrace. She loved her son dearly and had no idea just how ugly other people thought he was.

"Indeed," agreed his father. "I'll never have the honor of going to the palace."

"It is thanks to you both that I am here today," said Kui. "There were many times when you needed me to work in the fields but left me to my studies. I can never repay you."

"You already have," beamed his father. "Your success is our reward. You are about to meet the emperor of all China. Who knows where this might lead?"

Who indeed? Kui presented himself at the palace and was taken to the steps where he would wait to be received by the emperor.

When the emperor appeared, Kui kowtowed before him. This was a low and respectful bow–so low, in fact, that Kui's forehead touched the cold marble floor of the palace.

"Rise," said the emperor.

As Kui straightened up, their eyes met for the fist time. The emperor's imperial jaw dropped in horror and amazement. He refused to believe that anyone so ugly could really be the top student in the whole empire!

"Do you mean to tell me that this . . . this . . . *person* is the most clever?" he sputtered. "There has been some mistake! Take him out of my sight!"

So Kui bowed low and backed out of the palace in silence.

What could he tell his mother and father? He should, of course, have felt angry at the unfairness of it all–but instead, he felt ashamed.

Today was supposed to have been such a magnificent one for him and his family. Now it had turned into a day of rejection and shame.

Kui felt so downhearted and hopeless that he decided to kill himself. Without a second thought he hurled himself into the sea.

Kui may have been good at exams, but he was not so good at trying to take his own life. There was a mighty splash, and he landed on the head of a passing turtle, called Ao.

Perhaps gods were already at work. Or perhaps it really was simply a piece of good fortune for the scholar.

Startled, the turtle looked up and saw a man who wouldn't have looked out of place among his turtle friends. He decided, therefore, to steer this strange being to safety, which was extremely generous of him because Kui's clumsiness had given the poor creature a splitting headache.

The giant turtle soared out of the water, and because he was no ordinary sea creature, he continued to rise, carrying Kui higher and higher into the air. The startled expression on the scholar's face made him look even more extraordinary as he was carried all the way to Heaven.

There Kui became God of Examinations. He was one of two assistant gods to the God of Literature, Wen Chang. Although he was only Wen Chang's assistant, Kui was far more popular than the God of Literature. Shrines to Kui appeared in most houses where members of the family were about to take an exam.

Wen Chang may have been a more important god in the scheme of things, and was certainly better looking with his neatly trimmed mustache, but it was Kui who chose which candidates received top marks–so no wonder people wanted to please him.

The other assistant to Wen Chang was a god called Red Jacket. Red Jacket's role was to help some students who hadn't worked quite so hard as the others—ones who could never hope to get the higher marks, but who certainly didn't want to fail. But he only helped some of them because he, too, was a little lazy! In contrast, Kui would help every deserving candidate who prayed to him.

And what became of Ao, the giant turtle that had saved Kui's life? He was not forgotten. A likeness of his head was carved into the steps of the palace, and all candidates receiving honors from the emperor had to stand on it. The emperor would then announce: "May you alone stand upon the head of Ao."

As God of Literature, Wen Chang sometimes helped students, too. Once a clever candidate came home after an examination, convinced that he could have done better.

"I'm going to fail!" he groaned. "After months—years—of work, I know I could have done better. . . . If only I could sit down and retake the exam." And he prayed to Wen Chang. Nothing happened, and the boy went to bed depressed. He drifted off to sleep, and the God of Literature appeared to him in a dream.

The images were so clear and the colors were so vivid, it was as if the god was really there . . . as if the boy wasn't asleep at all. Wen Chang opened a stove and began to feed the flames with the essays from that morning's exam. The boy could see his own work among them.

When the papers had burned away, Wen Chang put his hand in the stove and crumbled the ashes together. He then pulled out an essay made up of the best parts of all the burned essays. He handed this to the boy, who read it and, thinking it brilliant, read it again, memorizing it word by word.

The next morning the student woke to hear his best friend banging on the door.

"What is it?" he asked.

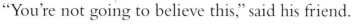

"You're not going to believe this," said his friend.

"What?"

"Bad news," said his friend.

"What?" repeated the student impatiently.

"We're going to have to take yesterday's exam all over again!"

"Why?" asked the puzzled student.

"Because the place where they were storing the papers was burned to the ground!" his friend explained.

The boy couldn't believe it. This wasn't *bad* news. It was quite the opposite, in fact. News couldn't get much better than this! His friend couldn't understand why he was grinning from ear to ear.

They retook the exam, and the boy wrote the essay Wen Chang had given him in his dream. His prayers had been answered. He passed with his best mark ever.

Kui, Red Jacket, and their master, Wen Chang, all live in Heaven in the constellation we know as the Great Bear. They still help students, and Kui's story is a good reminder that looks most definitely aren't everything.

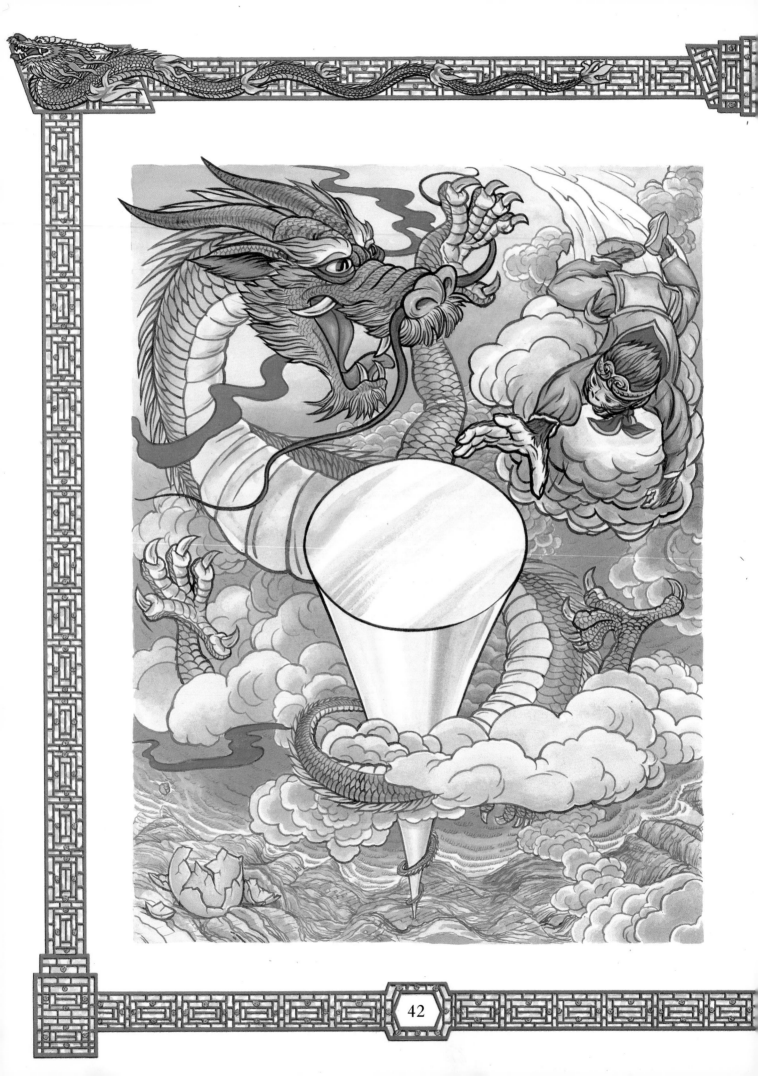

THE ADVENTURES OF MONKEY

More than a thousand years ago, a Chinese Buddhist monk called Xuan Zang (also known as Tripitaka) traveled to India to gather copies of Buddhist scriptures. His journey became a legend in which he traveled with someone called Monkey. Who was this mysterious being?

There had been a great stone egg resting on the slopes of Aolai Mountain on the shores of the Eastern Sea since the world began. It had been put there by the giant Pan Gu himself. Pan Gu was the first living being. His eyes became the sun and moon, his breath became the wind, and his voice thunder. His blood became the flowing rivers, and his veins were the many roads and pathways. His fleas became the human race.

One day the stone egg hatched and out jumped Monkey. He looked like an ordinary monkey and went to live in the mountains among the other monkeys. But they soon realized that he was not really like them. All monkeys are cunning, but he was the most cunning of them all. They made him their king.

Monkey was pleased to be king, and he ruled for many years. But after a few hundred years—some say one hundred, others say three hundred—Monkey realized that he would die one day, and he wondered what his subjects would do without him in charge.

He had heard stories of the Buddha and had learned that those who were truly enlightened and followed him were supposed to be able to live forever.

"If that works for humans, it should work for me!" said Monkey. And off he went to the world of humans to find himself a teacher –a master–to show him the way to immortality.

Monkey was a good student and a quick learner. By the end of his years of training in the ways of enlightenment, he could turn himself into anything he wanted to be, or fly through the skies on a cloud. He had also found the way to live forever.

Monkey returned home happy, only to find that the other monkeys were living in fear of a dreadful monster that had been terrorizing them while he had been gone. With his new powers Monkey was able to defeat the beast and its followers, but afterward he realized that this would have been a much easier task if he had had a special weapon.

He knew that the Dragon King of the Eastern Sea, where he had been born, guarded a pillar of iron. In the blinking of an eye, it could become a tiny needle, a column reaching from the ground to Heaven, or a fighting staff. This would make a very useful weapon indeed . . . so Monkey stole it from the dragon and kept it behind his ear for emergencies. He also had a magic cudgel–a great big club–that he liked to wave above his head to taunt his enemies.

With his new-found knowledge and strength, Monkey settled down to a peaceful life among his fellow monkeys. But one day, in the middle of a feast, two guards from the Underworld appeared. It was their job to lead souls to the Underworld to die at their allotted time.

"We have come for you," they said to Monkey.

"But I'm supposed to live forever!" he protested.

Monkey was so angry that he hit both of the guards over the head and then flew off to the Underworld in a terrible rage. He burst into the courts of Hell and demanded to see the Register of the Dead.

When he looked in the book, Monkey discovered that the guards had been telling the truth—he was indeed due to die that day. Shaking with anger, he took a brush and crossed out his name.

The Lord of the Underworld complained to the chief god, the Jade Emperor. The Jade Emperor had already had complaints about Monkey from the Dragon King, so he decided he must act quickly.

He knew that there was one thing Monkey wanted more than anything else: He wanted to be important. So the Jade Emperor offered Monkey a job with an important-sounding title: Keeper of the Heavenly Horse.

Monkey was very proud to accept, unaware that the emperor simply wanted him up in Heaven so he could keep an eye on him. It soon dawned on Monkey, though, just how unimportant this job was. He was about to get up to some of his old mischief-making when he was offered an even more important-sounding role: Great Sage, Equal of Heaven. But again, this was an important-sounding unimportant job.

Finally Monkey was given a job that really was important. He was made Guardian of the Garden of Immortal Peaches. This wasn't a very good idea because, as their name suggests, these were no ordinary peaches. This was the fruit eaten by the Immortals to make sure that they would live forever. It took 6,000 years for the crop of peaches to ripen. After these had been eaten, it would be another 6,000 years before the next crop was ripe enough to eat.

"What harm can I do eating just one?" thought Monkey. It was so delicious that he quickly followed it with another and another and another. By the time a group of maiden spirits arrived to pick the fruit for the Immortals' feast, Monkey was fast asleep in one of the trees, snoring loudly.

It didn't take much for the spirits to guess what had happened, with so many peaches missing and Monkey up a tree with peach pits scattered on the ground below him. They hurried off to tell Xiwangmu, the Queen of the West, who owned the garden.

When the queen heard the news, she was so angry that she decided not to invite Monkey to the feast with the other Immortals.

When Monkey heard this, he decided to eat most of the remaining peaches, as well as the wine he'd found in some gourds.

What he didn't realize was that this was the Elixir of Immortality, that Lao Zi–the founder of Taoism–was bringing to the feast. Monkey drank every last drop. Then he fell into an even deeper sleep.

When Monkey woke up later, he was filled with a terrible guilt. He hurried back to his mountain home among the monkeys and hoped that the gods wouldn't find him.

When the Jade Emperor was told of the unforgivable things Monkey had done this time, his patience ran out. He sent an army of 100,000 heavenly soldiers to capture him. There was battle after battle, and when Monkey was finally caught and taken to the Jade Emperor, there was no way that he could be sentenced to death. Monkey had eaten so many of the peaches and drunk so much of the elixir that he would live forever.

Instead the Jade Emperor ordered that Monkey be put into Lao Zi's furnace, where he would be melted into different parts, so even though he would still be alive, he wouldn't be able to do any harm. But when, after 49 days, the doors to the furnace were opened, Monkey jumped out, rubbing his eyes.

"Smoky in there!" he commented and then dashed off with a chattering monkey's laugh.

The Jade Emperor was desperate. Was there no way to calm this troublemaker? He decided to ask the Buddha for help. Buddha picked up Monkey by the scruff of the neck and placed him in his hand.

"If you can jump out of my hand, Monkey, I will make you the ruler of Heaven in the place of the Jade Emperor," he said. "If you can't, you must return to Earth and work hard to earn your right to live forever."

"Fair enough," grinned Monkey. He leaped high in the air and, after a long, long fall, landed at the foot of five huge pillars that were so tall that the tops disappeared into the mist far, far above.

"That was easy!" he laughed, and plucking out one of his hairs and using it as a brush, he wrote his name at the bottom of the middle pillar.

When he found Buddha looking down at him, Monkey claimed his right to rule Heaven.

"But you never left my hand," said Buddha.

"Oh, yes, I did," said Monkey indignantly, and told Buddha about the pillars and writing his name.

It was Buddha's turn to smile.

"Those five pillars were my five fingers," he said. "Look."

And, when he looked closely, Monkey could make out the word *MONKEY* at the base of Buddha's middle finger. He sighed. He had been defeated at last.

But Monkey's adventures had only just begun. As assistant to the Buddhist monk Xuan Zang, he soon became the hero of a series of amazing escapades. These are told in a famous sixteenth-century book called *Journey to the West*, **and they are still some of the most popular stories in China.**

Myths and Legends Resources

Here is just a sampling of other resources to look for. These resources on myths and legends are broken down into groups. Enjoy!

General Mythology

The Children's Dictionary of Mythology *edited by David Leeming* (Franklin Watts, 1999). This volume is a dictionary of terms, names, and places in the mythology of various cultures around the world.

Creation Read-aloud Stories from Many Lands *retold by Ann Pilling* (Candlewick Press, 1997). This is a collection of sixteen stories retold in an easy style and presented in three general groups: beginnings, warmth and light, and animals.

The Crystal Pool: Myths and Legends of the World *by Geraldine McCaughrean* (Margaret K. McElderry Books, 1998). Twenty-eight myths and legends from around the world comprise this book. They include the Chinese legend "The Alchemist" and the Celtic legend "Culloch and the Big Pig."

Encyclopedia Mythica
http://www.pantheon.org/areas/mythology/
From this page of the *Encyclopedia Mythica* site you can select from any of five countries to have the mythology of that area displayed.

A Family Treasury of Myths from Around the World *retold by Viviane Koenig* (Abrams, 1998). This collection of ten stories includes myths from Egypt, Africa, Greece, and other places around the world.

Goddesses, Heroes and Shamans: The Young People's Guide to World Mythology *edited by Cynthia O'Neill and others* (Kingfisher, 1994). This book introduces the reader to over five hundred mythological characters from around the world.

Gods, Goddesses and Monsters: An Encyclopedia of World Mythology *retold by Sheila Keenan* (Scholastic, 2000). This beautifully illustrated book discusses the characters and themes of the myths of peoples from Asia to Africa, to North and South America.

The Golden Hoard: Myths and Legends of the World *retold by Geraldine McCaughrean* (Margaret K. McElderry Books, 1995). This book contains twenty-two myths and legends that are exciting, adventurous, magical, and poetic.

The Illustrated Book of Myths: Tales and Legends of the World *retold by Neil Philips* (Dorling Kindersley, 1995). This beautifully illustrated collection brings together many of the most popular of the Greek and Roman, Norse, Celtic, Egyptian, Native American, African, and Indian myths.

Kids Zone: Myths and Fables from Around the World
http://www.afroam.org/children/myths/myths.html
Just click on your choice of the sixteen stories listed, and it will appear in full text.

Legends http://www.planetozkids.com/oban/legends.htm
From this Web page you can get the full text of any of the many listings.

Mythical Birds and Beasts from Many Lands *retold by Margaret Mayo* (Dutton, 1996). This book is a collection of stories that illustrate the special powers of birds and beasts that have become a part of folklore around the world.

Mythology *by Neil Philip* (Alfred A. Knopf, 1999). This superbly illustrated volume from the "Eyewitness Books" series surveys the treatment of such topics as gods and goddesses, the heavens, creation, the elements, and evil as expressed in various mythologies around the world.

Mythology *CD-ROM for Mac and Windows* (Thomas S. Klise, 1996). Educational games and puzzles, a glossary, and a testing section are all part of this CD introduction to Greek and Roman mythology.

Myths and Legends *by Neil Philip* (DK Publishing, 1999). More than fifty myths and legends from around the world are explained through works of art, text, and annotation by one of the world's foremost experts on mythology and folklore.

**The New York Public Library Amazing Mythology:
A Book of Answers for Kids** by *Brendan January*
(John Wiley, 2000). Over two hundred questions and
answers introduce myths from many ancient cultures,
including Egyptian, Greek, Roman, Celtic, Norse, and
Native American.

Plays from Mythology: Grades 4-6 by *L.E. McCullough*
(Smith and Kraus, 1998). Twelve original plays are
included, each with suggestions for staging and costumes.

Sources for Mythology
http://www.best.com/~atta/mythsrcs.html
In addition to defining mythology and distinguishing
it from legend and folklore, this Web site lists primary
sources for myths from many regions of the world,
as well as magazines, dictionaries, and other resources
relating to mythology.

Sun, Moon and Stars *retold by Mary Hoffman*
(Dutton, 1998). More than twenty myths and legends
from around the world, all explaining what was seen
in the sky, make up this exquisitely illustrated book.

AFRICAN

African Gods and their Associates
http://www3.sympatico.ca/untangle/africang.html
This Web page gives you a list of the African gods
with links to further information about them.

African Myths
http://www.cybercomm.net/~grandpa/africanmyths.html
Full text of several tales from the Kenya, Hausa, Ashanti,
and Nyanja tribes are included in this Web site.

Anansi and the Talking Melon *retold by Eric A. Kimmel*
(Holiday House, 1994). Anansi, a legendary character
from Africa, tricks Elephant and some other animals into
thinking that the melon in which he is hiding can talk.

Children's Stories from Africa *4 Video recordings (VHS)*
(Monterey Home Video, 1997). Among the African
Legends on this page: "How the Hare Got His Long
Legs," "How the Porcupine Got His Quills," "The Brave
Sititunga," and "The Greedy Spider."

**The Hero with an African Face: Mythic Wisdom
of Traditional Africa** by *Clyde W. Ford* (Bantam, 2000).
"The Hero with an African Face" is only one of the
several stories included in this book, which also includes
a map of the peoples and myths of Africa and a
pronunciation guide for African words.

Kings, Gods and Spirits from African Mythology
retold by Jan Knappert (Peter Bedrick Books, 1993). This
illustrated collection contains myths and legends of the
peoples of Africa.

Legends of Africa by *Mwizenge Tembo* (Metro Books,
1996). This indexed and illustrated volume is from the
"Myths of the World" series.

Myths and Legends *retold by O. B. Duane* (Brockhampton
Press, 1998). Duane has vividly retold some of the most
gripping African tales.

CELTIC

Celtic Myths *retold by Sam McBratney* (Peter Bedrick,
1997). This collection of fifteen illustrated stories draws
from English, Irish, Scottish, and Welsh folklore.

Excalibur *retold by Hudson Talbott* (Books of Wonder,
1996). In this illustrated story from the legends of King
Arthur, Arthur receives his magical sword, Excalibur

Irish Fairy Tales and Legends *retold by Una Leavy*
(Robert Rinehart, 1996). Cuchulainn, Deirdre, and
Fionn Mac Cumhail are only three of the legendary
characters you will meet in this volume.

Irish Myths and Legends
http://www.mc.maricopa.edu/users/shoemaker/
    Celtic/index.html
This Web site is for those more serious in their
study of Irish myths and legends.

King Arthur by *Rosalind Kerven* (DK Publishing, 1998).
This book from the "Eyewitness Classic" series is a
retelling of the boy who was fated to be the "Once and
Future King" It includes illustrated notes to explain the
historical background of the story.

Robin Hood and His Merry Men *retold by Jane Louise*
Curry (Margaret K. McElderry, 1994). This collection
contains seven short stories of the legendary hero
Robin Hood, who lived with his band of followers in
Sherwood Forest.

**The World of King Arthur and his Court: People,
Places, Legend and Love** by *Kevin Crossley-Holland*
(Dutton, 1998). The author combines legend, anecdote,
fact, and speculation to help answer some of the questions regarding King Arthur and his chivalrous world.

CHINESE

Asian Mythology by *Rachel Storm* (Lorenz, 2000).
Included in this volume are myths and legends of China.

Chinese Culture
http://chineseculture.about.com/culture/
    chineseculture/msub82.htm
Use this Web page as a starting point for further
exploration about Chinese myths and legends.

Chinese Mythology by *Anne Birrell* (Johns Hopkins, 1999). This comprehensive introduction to Chinese mythology will meet the needs of the more serious and the general reader

Chinese Myths and Legends *retold by O. B. Duane and others* (Brockhampton Press, 1998). Introductory notes by the author give further explanation of the thirty-eight stories included in this illustrated volume.

Dragons and Demons by *Stewart Ross* (Cooper Beech, 1998). Included in this collection of myths and legends from Asia are the Chinese myths "Chang Lung the Dragon" and "The Ugly Scholar."

Dragons, Gods and Spirits from Chinese Mythology *retold by Tao Tao Liu Sanders* (Peter Bedrick Books, 1994). The stories in this book include ancient myths about nature, the gods, and creation as well as religious legends.

Fa Mulan: The Story of a Woman Warrior *retold by Robert D. San Souci* (Hyperion, 1998). Artists Jean and Mou-Sien Tseng illustrate this Chinese legend of a young heroine who is courageous, selfless, and wise.

Land of the Dragon: Chinese Myth by *Tony Allan* (Time-Life, 1999). This volume from the "Myth and Mankind" series includes many of China's myths as well as examination of the myth and its historical roots.

Selected Chinese Myths and Fantasies
http://www.chinavista.com/experience/story/story.html
From this Web site and its links you will find several Chinese myths that are enjoyed by children as well as the history of Chinese mythology.

EGYPTIAN

Egyptian Gods and Goddesses by *Henry Barker* (Grosset and Dunlap, 1999). In this book designed for the young reader, religious beliefs of ancient Egypt are discussed, as well as their gods and goddesses.

Egyptian Mythology A-Z: A Young Reader's Companion by *Pat Remler* (Facts on File, 2000). Alphabetically arranged, this resource defines words relating to Egyptian mythology.

Egyptian Myths *retold by Jacqueline Morley* (Peter Bedrick Books, 1999). Legends of the pharaohs, myths about creation, and the search for the secret of all knowledge, make up this illustrated book.

The Gods and Goddesses of Ancient Egypt by *Leonard Everett Fisher* (Holiday House, 1997). This artist/writer describes thirteen of the most important Egyptian gods.

Gods and Myths of Ancient Egypt by *Mary Barnett* (Regency House, 1996). Beautiful color photographs are used to further explain the text in this summary of Egyptian mythology.

Gods and Pharaohs from Egyptian Mythology *retold by Geraldine Harris* (Peter Bedrick Books, 1992). The author gives some background information about the Ancient Egyptians and then retells more than twenty of their myths.

Myth Man's Egyptian Homework Help
http://egyptmyth.com/
Cool Facts and Fun for Kids and *Egyptian Myth Encyclopedia* are only two of the many wonderful links this page will lead you to.

Myths and Civilizations of the Ancient Egyptians by *Sarah Quie* (Peter Bedrick Books, 1998). The author intersperses Egypt's myths with a history of its civilization in this illustrated volume.

The Secret Name of Ra *retold by Anne Rowe* (Rigby Interactive Library, 1996). In this Egyptian myth, Isis tricks Ra into revealing his secret name so that she and her husband Osiris can become rulers of the earth.

Tales from Ancient Egypt *retold by George Hart* (Hoopoe Books, 1994). The seven tales in this collection include stories of animals, of Isis and Horus, of a sailor lost on a magic island, and of pharaohs and their magicians.

Who's Who in Egyptian Mythology by *Anthony S. Mercatante* (Scarecrow Press, 1995). The author has compiled a concise, easy-to-use dictionary of ancient Egyptian deities.

GREEK

Aίίta and the Queen: A Tale of Ancient Greece by *Priscilla Galloway* (Annick Press, 1995). This made-up story, which is based on Homer's epic poem, *The Odyssey*, reads like a novel.

Cupid and Psyche *retold by M. Charlotte Craft* (Morrow Junior Books, 1996). This classic love story from Greek mythology will appeal to young and old.

Gods and Goddesses by *John Malam* (Peter Bedrick Books, 1999). This volume is packed with information about the important gods and goddesses of ancient Greece, including Zeus, Hera, Athena, and Hades.

Greek and Roman Mythology by *Dan Nardo* (Lucent, 1998). The author examines the historical development of Greco-Roman mythology, its heroes, and its influence on the history of Western civilization.

Guide for Using D'Aulaires' Book of Greek Myths in the Classroom by *Cynthia Ross* (Teacher Created Materials, 1993). This reproducible book includes sample plans, author information, vocabulary-building ideas, cross-curricular activities, quizzes, and many ideas for extending this classic work.

Hercules by *Robert Burleigh* (Harcourt Brace, 1999). Watercolor and color pencil illustrations help to tell the story of Hercules's final labor in which he went back to the underworld and brought back the three-headed dog, Cerberus.

Medusa by *Deborah Nourse Lattimire* (Joanna Cotler Books, 2000). The author/illustrator of this book re-creates the tragedy of one of the best-known Greek myths, the tale of the beautiful Medussa whose conceit causes a curse be placed on her.

The Myths and Legends of Ancient Greece *CD-ROM for Mac and Windows* (Clearvue, 1996). This CD conveys the heroic ideals and spirit of Greek mythology as it follows ten of the best-known myths.

Mythweb http://www.mythweb.com/ This Web page provides links to Greek gods, heroes, an encyclopedia of mythology, and teacher resources.

Pegasus, the Flying Horse *retold by Jane Yolen* (Dutton, 1998). This Greek myth tells of how Bellerophon, with the help of Athena, tames the winged horse Pegasus and conquers the monstrous Chimaera.

The Race of the Golden Apples *retold by Claire Martin* (Dial, 1991). Caldecott Medal winners Leo and Diane Dillon have illustrated this myth of Atalanta, the beautiful Greek princess.

The Random House Book of Greek Myths by *Joan D. Vinge* (Random House, 1999). The author retells some of the famous Greek myths about gods, goddesses, humans, heroes, and monsters, explaining the background of the tales and why these tales have survived.

The Robber Baby: Stories from the Greek Myths *retold by Anne Rockwell* (Greenwillow Books, 1994). Anne Rockwell, a well-known name in children's literature, has put together a superbly retold collection of myths that will be enjoyed by readers of all ages.

NORSE

Beowulf by *Welwyn Wilton Katz* (Groundwood, 2000). The illustrations in this classic legend are based on the art of the Vikings.

Favorite Norse Myths *retold by Mary Pope Osborne* (Scholastic, 1996). These fourteen tales of Norse gods, goddesses, and giants are based on the oldest written sources of Norse mythology, *Prose Edda* and *Poetic Edda*.

The Giant King by *Rosalind Kerven* (NTC Publishing Group, 1998). Photos of artifacts from the Viking Age illustrate these two stories that are rooted in Norse mythology.

Gods and Heroes from Viking Mythology by *Brian Branston* (Peter Bedrick Books, 1994). This illustrated volume tells the stories of Thor, Balder, King Gylfi, and other Nordic gods and goddesses

Handbook of Norse Mythology by *John Lindow* (Ambcc, 2001). For the advanced reader, this handbook covers the tales, their literary and oral sources, includes an A-to-Z of the key mythological figures, concepts and events, and so much more.

Kids Domain Fact File http://www.kidsdomain.co.uk/teachers/resources/ fact_file_viking_gods_and_goddesses.html This child-centered Web page is a dictionary of Viking gods and goddesses.

Myths and Civilization of the Vikings by *Hazel Martell* (Peter Bedrick, 1998). Each of the nine stories in this book is followed by a non-fiction spread with information about Viking society.

Norse Mythology: The Myths and Legends of the Nordic Gods *retold by Arthur Cotterell* (Lorenz Books, 2000). This encyclopedia of the Nordic peoples' myths and legends is generously illustrated with fine art paintings of the classic stories.

Odins' Family: Myths of the Vikings *retold by Neil Philip* (Orchard Books, 1996). This collection of stories of Odin, the All-father, and the other Viking gods Thor, Tyr, Frigg, and Loer is full of excitement that encompasses both tragedy and comedy.

Stolen Thunder: A Norse Myth *retold by Shirley Climo* (Houghton Mifflin, 1994). This story, beautifully illustrated by Alexander Koshkin, retells the Norse myth about the god of Thunder and the recovery of his magic hammer Mjolnir, from the Frost Giany, Thrym.

NORTH AMERICAN

Buffalo Dance: A Blackfoot Legend *retold by Nancy Can Laan* (Little, Brown and Company, 1993). This illustrated version of the Native North American legend tells of the ritual performed before the buffalo hunt.

The Favorite Uncle Remus *by Joel Chandler Harris* (Houghton Mifflin, 1948). This classic work of literature is a collection of stories about Brer Rabbit, Brer Fox, Brer Tarrypin, and others that were told to the author as he grew up in the South.

Iktomi Loses his Eyes: A Plains Indian Story *retold by Paul Goble* (Orchard Books, 1999). The legendary character Iktomi finds himself in a predicament after losing his eyes when he misuses a magical trick.

The Legend of John Henry *retold by Terry Small* (Doubleday, 1994). This African American legendary character, a steel driver on the railroad, pits his strength and speed against the new steam engine hammer that is putting men out of jobs.

The Legend of the White Buffalo Woman *retold by Paul Goble* (National Geographic Society, 1998). This Native American Plains legend tells the story of the White Buffalo Woman who gave her people the Sacred Calf Pipe so that people would pray and commune with the Great Spirit.

Myths and Legends for American Indian Youth http://www.kstrom.net/isk/stories/myths.html Stories from Native Americans across the United States are included in these pages.

Snail Girl Brings Water: a Navajo Story *retold by Geri Keams* (Rising Moon, 1998). This retelling of a traditional Navajo re-creation myth explains how water came to earth.

The Woman Who Fell from the Sky: The Iroquois Story of Creation *retold by John Bierhirst* (William Morrow, 1993). This myth describes how the creation of the world was begun by a woman who fell down to earth from the sky country, and how it was finished by her two sons.

SOUTH AMERICAN (INCLUDING CENTRAL AMERICAN)

Gods and Goddesses of the Ancient Maya *by Leonard Everett Fisher* (Holiday House, 1999). With text and illustration inspired by the art, glyphs, and sculpture of the ancient Maya, this artist and author describes twelve of the most important Maya gods.

How Music Came to the World: An Ancient Mexican Myth *retold by Hal Ober* (Houghton Mifflin, 1994). This illustrated book, which includes author notes and a pronunciation guide, is an Aztec pourquoi story that explains how music came to the world.

Llama and the Great Flood *retold by Ellen Alexander* (Thomas Y. Crowell, 1989). In this illustrated retelling of the Peruvian myth about the Great Flood, a llama warns his master of the coming destruction and leads him and his family to refuge on a high peak in the Andes.

The Legend of the Poinsettia *retold by Tomie dePaola* (G. P. Putnam's Sons,1994). This beautifully illustrated Mexican legend tells of how the poinsettia came to be when a young girl offered her gift to the Christ child.

Lost Realms of Gold: South American Myth *edited by Tony Allan* (Time-Life Books, 2000). This volume, which captures the South American mythmakers' fascination with magic, includes the tale of the first Inca who built the city of Cuzco, as well as the story of the sky people who discovered the rain forest.

People of Corn: A Mayan Story *retold by Mary-Joan Gerson* (Little, Brown, 1995). In this richly illustrated creation story, the gods first try and fail, then try and fail again before they finally succeed.

Tales from the Rain Forest: Myths and Legends from the Amazonian Indians of Brazil *retold by Mercedes Dorson* (Ecco Press, 1997). Ten stories from this region include "The Origin of Rain" and "How the Stars Came to Be."

WHO'S WHO IN MYTHS AND LEGENDS

This is a cumulative listing of some important characters found in all eight volumes of the **World Book Myths and Legends** series.

A

Aegir (EE jihr), also called Hler, was the god of the sea and the husband of Ran in Norse myths. He was lord of the undersea world where drowned sailors spent their days.

Amma (ahm mah) was the creator of the world in the myths of the Dogon people of Africa. Mother Earth was his wife, and Water and Light were his children. Amma also created the people of the world.

Amun (AH muhn), later Amun-Ra, became the king of gods in later Egyptian myths. Still later he was seen as another form of Ra.

Anubis (uh NOO bihs) in ancient Egypt was the god of the dead and helper to Osiris. He had the head of a jackal.

Ao (ow) was a giant turtle in a Chinese myth. He saved the life of Kui.

Aphrodite (af ruh DY tee) in ancient Greece was the goddess of love. She was known for her beauty. The Romans called her Venus.

Arianrod (air YAN rohd) in Welsh legends was the mother of the hero Llew.

Arthur (AHR thur) in ancient Britain was the king of the Britons. He probably was a real person who ruled long before the age of knights in armor. His queen was Guinevere.

Athena (uh THEE nuh) in ancient Greece was the goddess of war. The Romans called her Minerva.

Atum (AH tuhm) was the creator god of ancient Egypt and the father of Shu and Tefnut. He later became Ra-Atum.

B

Babe (bayb) in North American myths was the big blue ox owned by Paul Bunyan.

Balder (BAWL dur) was the god of light in Norse myths. He was the most handsome of all gods and was Frigga's favorite son.

Balor (BAL awr) was an ancient chieftain in Celtic myths who had an evil eye. He fought Lug, the High King of Ireland.

Ban Hu (bahn hoo) was the dog god in a myth that tells how the Year of the Dog in the Chinese calendar got its name.

Bastet (BAS teht), sometimes Bast (bast) in ancient Egypt was the mother goddess. She was often shown as a cat. Bastet was the daughter of Ra and the sister of Hathor and Sekhmet.

Bellerophon (buh LEHR uh fahn) in ancient Greek myths was a hero who captured and rode the winged horse, Pegasus.

Blodeuwedd was the wife of Llew in Welsh legends. She was made of flowers woven together by magic.

Botoque (boh toh kay) in Kayapó myths was the boy who first ate cooked meat and told people about fire.

Brer Rabbit (brair RAB iht) was a clever trickster rabbit in North American myths.

C

Chameleon (kuh MEEL yuhn) in a Yoruba myth of Africa was a messenger sent to trick the god Olokun and teach him a lesson.

Conchobar (KAHN koh bahr), also called Conor, was the king of Ulster. He was a villain in many Irish myths.

Coyote (ky OH tee) was an evil god in myths of the Maidu and some other Native American people.

Crow (kroh) in Inuit myths was the wise bird who brought daylight to the Inuit people.

Cuchulain (koo KUHL ihn), also Cuchullain or Cuchulan, in Irish myths was Ireland's greatest warrior of all time. He was the son of Lug and Dechtire.

Culan (KOO luhn) in Irish myths was a blacksmith. His hound was killed by Setanta, who later became Cuchulain.

D

Davy Crockett (DAY vee KRAHK iht) was a real person. He is remembered as an American frontier hero who died in battle and also in legends as a great hunter and woodsman.

Dechtire (DEHK teer) in Irish myths was the sister of King Conchobar and mother of Cuchulain.

Deirdre (DAIR dray) in Irish myths was the daughter of Fedlimid. She refused to wed Conchobar. It was said that she would lead to Ireland's ruin.

Di Jun (dee joon) was god of the Eastern Sky in Chinese myths. He lived in a giant mulberry tree.

Di Zang Wang (dee zahng wahng) in Chinese myths was a Buddhist monk who was given that name when he became the lord of the underworld. His helper was Yan Wang, god of the dead.

Dionysus (dy uh NY suhs) was the god of wine in ancient Greek myths. He carried a staff wrapped in vines.

Dolapo was the wife of Kigbo in a Yoruba myth of Africa.

E

Eight Immortals (ihm MAWR tuhlz) in Chinese myths were eight ordinary human beings whose good deeds led them to truth and enlightenment. The Eight Immortals were godlike heroes. They had special powers to help people.

El Niño (ehl NEEN yoh) in Inca myths was the ruler of the wind, the weather, and the ocean and its creatures.

Emer (AYV ur) in Irish myths was the daughter of Forgal the Wily and wife of Cuchulain.

F

Fafnir (FAHV nihr) in Norse myths was a son of Hreidmar. He killed his father for his treasure, sent his brother Regin away, and turned himself into a dragon.

Frey (fray), also called Freyr, was the god of summer in Norse myths. His chariot was pulled by a huge wild boar.

Freya (FRAY uh) was the goddess of beauty and love in Norse myths. Her chariot was pulled by two large cats.

Frigga (FRIHG uh), also called Frigg, in Norse myths was the wife of Odin and mother of many gods. She was the most powerful goddess in Asgard.

Frog was an animal prince in an Alur myth of Africa. He and his brother, Lizard, competed for the right to inherit the throne of their father.

Fu Xi (foo shee) in a Chinese myth was a boy who, with his sister Nü Wa, freed the Thunder God and was rewarded. His name means Gourd Boy.

G

Gaunab was Death, who took on a human form in a Khoi myth of Africa. Tsui'goab fought with Gaunab to save his people.

Geb (gehb) in ancient Egypt was the Earth itself. All plants and trees grew from his back. He was the brother and husband of Nut and the father of the gods Osiris, Isis, Seth, and Nephthys.

Glooscap (glohs kap) was a brave and cunning god in the myths of Algonquian Native American people. He was a trickster who sometimes got tricked.

Guinevere (GWIHN uh vihr) in British and Welsh legends was King Arthur's queen, who was also loved by Sir Lancelot.

Gwydion (GWIHD ih uhn) in Welsh legends was the father of Llew and the nephew of the magician and ruler, Math.

H

Hades (HAY deez) in ancient Greece was the god of the dead. Hades was also called Pluto (PLOO toh). The Romans called him Dis.

Hairy Man was a frightening monster in African American folk tales.

Harpy (HAHRP ee) was one of the hideous winged women in Greek myths. The hero Jason and his Argonauts freed King Phineas from the harpies' power.

Hathor (HATH awr) was worshiped in the form of a cow in ancient Egypt, but she also appeared as an angry lioness. She was the daughter of Ra and the sister of Bastet and Sekhmet.

Heimdall (HAYM dahl) was the god in Norse myths who guarded the rainbow bridge joining Asgard, the home of the gods, to other worlds.

Hel (hehl), also called Hela, was the goddess of death in Norse myths. The lower half of her body was like a rotting corpse. Hel was Loki's daughter.

Helen (HEHL uhn), called Helen of Troy, was a real person in ancient Greece. According to legend, she was known as the most beautiful woman in the world. Her capture by Paris led to the Trojan War.

Heng E (huhng ay), sometimes called Chang E, was a woman in Chinese myths who became the moon goddess. She was the wife of Yi the Archer.

Hera (HEHR uh) in ancient Greece was the queen of heaven and the wife of Zeus. The Romans called her Juno.

Heracles (HEHR uh kleez) in ancient Greek myths was a hero of great strength. He was the son of Zeus. He had to complete twelve tremendous tasks in order to become one of the gods. The Romans called him Hercules.

Hermes (HUR meez) was the messenger of the gods in Greek myths. He wore winged sandals. The Romans called him Mercury.

Hoder (HOO dur) was Balder's twin brother in Norse myths. He was blind. It was said that after a mighty battle he and Balder would be born again.

Hoenir (HAY nihr), also called Honir, was a god in Norse myths. In some early myths, he is said to be Odin's brother.

Horus (HAWR uhs) in ancient Egypt was the son of Isis and Osiris. He was often shown with the head of a falcon. Horus fought Seth to rule Egypt.

Hreidmar (HRAYD mahr) was a dwarf king in Norse myths who held Odin for a huge pile of treasure. His sons were Otter, Fafnir, and Regin.

Hyrrokkin (HEER rahk kihn) in Norse myths was a terrifying female giant who rode an enormous wolf using poisonous snakes for reins.

I

Irin-Mage (eereen mah geh) in Tupinambá myths was the only person to be saved when the creator, Monan, destroyed the other humans. Irin-Mage became the ancestor of all people living today.

Isis (EYE sihs) in ancient Egypt was the goddess of fertility and a master of magic. She became the most powerful of all the gods and goddesses. She was the sister and wife of Osiris and mother of Horus.

J

Jade Emperor (jayd EHM puhr uhr) in Buddhist myths of China was the chief god in Heaven.

Jason (JAY suhn) was a hero in Greek myths. His ship was the Argo, and the men who sailed with him on his adventures were called the Argonauts.

Johnny Appleseed (AP uhl seed) was a real person, John Chapman. He is remembered in legends as the person who traveled across North America, planting apple orchards.

K

Kaboi (kah boy) was a very wise man in a Carajá myth. He helped his people find their way from their underground home to the surface of the earth.

Kewawkwuí (kay wow kwoo) were a group of powerful, frightening giants and magicians in the myths of Algonquian Native American people.

Kigbo (keeg boh) was a stubborn man in a Yoruba myth of Africa. His stubbornness got him into trouble with spirits.

Kodoyanpe (koh doh yahn pay) was a good god in the myths of the Maidu and some other Native American people. He was the brother of the evil god Coyote.

Kuang Zi Lian (kwahng dsee lee ehn) in a Taoist myth of China was a very rich, greedy farmer who was punished by one of the Eight Immortals.

Kui in Chinese myths was an ugly, brilliant scholar who became God of Examinations.

Kvasir (KVAH sihr) in Norse myths was the wisest of all the gods in Asgard.

L

Lancelot (lan suh laht) in British and Welsh legends was King Arthur's friend and greatest knight. He was secretly in love with Guinevere.

Lao Zi (low dzuh) was the man who founded the Chinese religion of Taoism. He wrote down the Taoist beliefs in a book, the *Tao Te Ching*.

Li Xuan (lee shwahn) was one of the Eight Immortals in ancient Chinese myths.

Light (lyt) was a child of Amma, the creator of the world, in a myth of the Dogon people of Africa.

Lizard (LIHZ urd) was an animal prince in an Alur myth of Africa. He was certain that he, and not his brother, Frog, would inherit the throne of their father.

Llew Llaw Gyffes (LE yoo HLA yoo GUHF ehs), also Lleu Law Gyffes, was a hero in Welsh myths who had many adventures. His mother was Arianrod and his father was Gwydion.

Loki (LOH kee) in Norse myths was a master trickster. His friends were Odin and Thor. Loki was half giant and half god, and could be funny and also cruel. He caused the death of Balder.

Lord of Heaven was the chief god in some ancient Chinese myths.

Lug (luk) in Irish myths was the Immortal High King of Ireland, Master of All Arts.

M

Maira-Monan (mah ee rah moh nahn) was the most powerful son of Irin-Mage in Tupinambá myths. He was destroyed by people who were afraid of his powers.

Manco Capac (mahn kih kah pahk) in Inca myths was the founder of the Inca people. He was one of four brothers and four sisters who led the Inca to their homeland.

Manitou (MAN ih toh) was the greatest and most powerful of all gods in Native American myths of the Iroquois people.

Math (mohth) in Welsh myths was a magician who ruled the Welsh kingdom of Gwynedd.

Michabo (mee chah boh) in the myths of Algonquian Native American people was the Great Hare, who taught people to hunt and brought them luck. He was a son of West Wind.

Monan (moh nahn) was the creator in Tupinambá myths.

Monkey (MUNG kee) is the hero of many Chinese stories. The most cunning of all monkeys, he became the king of monkeys and caused great troubles for the gods.

N

Nanook (na NOOK) was the white bear in myths of the Inuit people.

Naoise (NEE see) in Irish myths was Conchobar's nephew and the lover of Deirdre. He was the son of Usnech and brother of Ardan and Ainle.

Nekumonta (neh koo mohn tah) in Native American myths of the Iroquois people was a person whose goodness helped him save his people from a terrible sickness.

Nü Wa (nyuh wah) in a Chinese myth was a girl who, with her brother, Fu Xi, freed the Thunder God and was rewarded. Her name means Gourd Girl.

Nuada (NOO uh thuh) in Irish myths was King of the Tuatha Dé Danann, the rulers of all Ireland. He had a silver hand.

O

Odin (OH dihn), also called Woden, in Norse myths was the chief of all the gods and a brave warrior. He had only one eye. He was the husband of Frigga and father of many of the gods. His two advisers were the ravens Hugin and Munin.

Odysseus (oh DIHS ee uhs) was a Greek hero who fought in the Trojan War. The poet Homer wrote of his many adventures.

Oedipus (ED uh puhs) was a tragic hero in Greek myths. He unknowingly killed his own father and married his mother.

Olodumare (oh loh doo mah ray) was the supreme god in Yoruba myths of Africa.

Olokun (oh loh koon) was the god of water and giver of life in Yoruba myths of Africa. He challenged Olodumare for the right to rule.

Orpheus (AWR fee uhs) in Greek myths was famed for his music. He followed his wife, Euridice, to the kingdom of the dead to plead for her life.

Osiris (oh SY rihs) in ancient Egypt was the ruler of the dead in the kingdom of the West. He was the brother and husband of Isis and the father of Horus.

P

Pamola (pah moh lah) in the myths of Algonquian Native American people was an evil spirit of the night.

Pan Gu (pahn goo) in Chinese myths was the giant who was the first living being.

Pandora (pan DAWR uh) in ancient Greek myths was the first woman.

Paris (PAR ihs) was a real person, a hero from the city of Troy. He captured Helen, the queen of a Greek kingdom, and took her to Troy.

Paul Bunyan (pawl BUHN yuhn) was a tremendously strong giant lumberjack in North American myths.

Perseus (PUR see uhs) was a human hero in myths of ancient Greece. His most famous adventure was killing Medusa, a creature who turned anyone who looked at her to stone.

Poseidon (puh SY duhn) was the god of the sea in myths of ancient Greece. He carried a three-pronged spear called a trident to make storms and control the waves. The Romans called him Neptune.

Prometheus (pruh MEE thee uhs) was the cleverest of the gods in Greek myths. He was a friend to humankind.

Q

Queen Mother of the West was a goddess in Chinese myths.

R

Ra (rah), sometimes Re (ray), was the sun god of ancient Egypt. He was often shown with the head of a hawk. Re became the most important god. Other gods were sometimes combined with him and had Ra added to their names.

Ran (rahn) was the goddess of the sea in Norse myths. She pulled sailors from their boats in a large net and dragged them underwater.

Red Jacket in Chinese myths was an assistant to Wen Chang, the god of literature. His job was to help students who hadn't worked very hard.

S

Sekhmet (SEHK meht) in ancient Egypt was a bloodthirsty goddess with the head of a lioness. She was the daughter of Ra and the sister of Bastet and Hathor.

Setanta in Irish myths was Cuchulain's name before he killed the hound of Culan.

Seth (set), sometimes Set, in ancient Egypt was the god of chaos and confusion, who fought Horus to rule Egypt. He was the evil son of Geb and Nut.

Shanewis (shah nay wihs) in Native American myths of the Iroquois people was the wife of Nekumonta.

Shu (shoo) in ancient Egypt was the father of the sky goddess Nut. He held Nut above Geb, the Earth, to keep the two apart.

Sinchi Roca was the second emperor of the Inca. According to legend, he was the son of Ayar Manco (later known as Manco Capac) and his sister Mama Ocllo.

Skirnir (SKEER nihr) in Norse myths was a brave, faithful servant of the god Frey.

Sphinx (sfihngks) in Greek myths was a creature that was half lion and half woman, with eagle wings. It killed anyone who failed to answer its riddle.

T

Tefnut (TEHF noot) was the moon goddess in ancient Egypt. She was the sister and wife of Shu and the mother of Nut and Geb.

Theseus (THEE see uhs) was a human hero in myths of ancient Greece. He killed the Minotaur, a half-human, half-bull creature, and freed its victims.

Thor (thawr) was the god of thunder in Norse myths. He crossed the skies in a chariot pulled by goats and had a hammer, Mjollnir, and a belt, Meginjardir.

Thunder God (THUN dur gahd) in Chinese myths was the god of thunder and rain. He got his power from water and was powerless if he could not drink.

Tsui'goab (tsoo ee goh ahb) was the god of rain in myths of the Khoi people of Africa. He was a human who became a god after he fought to save his people.

Tupan (too pahn) was the spirit of thunder and lightning in Inca myths.

Tyr (tihr) was the god of war in Norse myths. He was the bravest god and was honorable and true, as well. He had just one hand.

U

Utgard-Loki (OOT gahrd LOH kee) in Norse myths was the clever, crafty giant king of Utgard. He once disguised himself as a giant called Skrymir to teach Thor a lesson.

W

Water God (WAW tur gahd) in Chinese myths was a god who sent rain and caused floods.

Wen Chang (wehn chuhng) in Chinese myths was the god of literature. His assistants were Kui and Red Jacket.

Wu (woo) was a lowly courtier in a Chinese myth who fell in love with a princess.

X

Xi He (shee heh) in Chinese myths was the goddess wife of Di Jun, the god of the eastern sky.

Xiwangmu (shee wahng moo) in Chinese myths was the owner of the Garden of Immortal Peaches.

Xuan Zang (shwahn dsahng), also called Tripitaka, was a real person, a Chinese Buddhist monk who traveled to India to gather copies of religious writings. Legends about him tell that Monkey was his traveling companion.

Y

Yan Wang (yahn wahng) was the god of the dead and judge of the first court of the Underworld in Chinese myths. He was helper to Di Zang Wang.

Yao (yow) was a virtuous emperor in Chinese myths. Because Yao lived simply and was a good leader, Yi the Archer was sent to help him.

Yi (yee) was an archer in Chinese myths who was sent by Di Jun to save the earth, in answer to Yao's prayers.

Z

Zeus (zoos) in ancient Greece was the king of gods and the god of thunder and lightning. The Romans called him Jupiter.

Zhao Shen Xiao (zhow shehn shi ow) in Chinese myths was a good magistrate, or official, who arrested the greedy merchant Kuang Zi Lian.

MYTHS AND LEGENDS GLOSSARY

This is a cumulative glossary of some important places and terms found in all eight volumes of the *World Book Myths and Legends* series.

A

Alfheim (AHLF hym) in Norse myth was the home of the light elves.

Asgard (AS gahrd) in Norse myths was the home of the warrior gods who were called the Aesir. It was connected to the earth by a rainbow bridge.

Augean (aw JEE uhn) stables were stables that the Greek hero Heracles had to clean as one of his twelve labors. He made the waters of two rivers flow through the stables and wash away the filth.

Avalon (AV uh lahn) in British legends was the island where King Arthur was carried after he died in battle. The legend says he will rise again to lead Britain.

B

Bard (bahrd) was a Celtic poet and singer in ancient times. A bard entertained people by making up and singing poems about brave deeds.

Battle of the Alamo (AL uh moh) was a battle between Texas settlers and Mexican forces when Texas was fighting for independence from Mexico. It took place at the Alamo, a fort in San Antonio, in 1836.

Bifrost (BEE fruhst) in Norse myths was a rainbow bridge that connected Asgard with the world of people.

Black Land in ancient Egypt was the area of fertile soil around the banks of the River Nile. Most people lived there.

Brer Rabbit (brair RAB iht) myths are African American stories about a rabbit who played tricks on his friends. The stories grew out of animal myths from Africa.

C

Canoe Mountain in a Maidu myth of North America was the mountain on which the evil Coyote took refuge from a flood sent to drown him.

Changeling (CHAYNG lihng) in Celtic myths was a fairy child who had been swapped with a human baby at birth. Changelings were usually lazy and clumsy.

Confucianism (kuhn FYOO shuhn IHZ uhm) is a Chinese way of life and religion. It is based on the teachings of Confucius, also known as Kong Fu Zi, and is more than 2,000 years old.

Creation myths (kree AY shuhn mihths) are myths that tell how the world began.

D

Dwarfs (dwawrfs) in Norse myths were small people of great power. They were skilled at making tools and weapons.

F

Fairies (FAIR eez) in Celtic myths were called the Little People. They are especially common in Irish legends, where they are called leprechauns.

Fomors (FOH wawrz) in Irish myths were hideous giants who invaded Ireland and were fought by Lug.

G

Giants (JY uhnts) in Norse myths were huge people who had great strength and great powers. They often struggled with the warrior gods of Asgard.

Gnome (nohm) was a small, odd-looking person in the myths of many civilizations. In Inca myths, for example, gnomes were tiny people with very big beards.

Golden Apples of the Hesperides (heh SPEHR uh deez) were apples of gold in a garden that only the Greek gods could enter. They were collected by the hero Heracles as one of his twelve labors.

Golden fleece was the fleece of a ram that the Greek hero Jason won after many adventures with his ship, Argo, and his companion sailors, the Argonauts.

Green Knoll (nohl) was the home of the Little People, or fairies, in Irish and Scottish myths.

J

Jotunheim (YUR toon hym) in Norse myths was the land of the giants.

L

Lion men in myths of Africa were humans who can turn themselves into lions.

Little People in Celtic legends and folk tales are fairies. They are often fine sword makers and blacksmiths.

M

Machu Picchu (MAH choo PEE choo) is the ruins of an ancient city built by the Inca in the Andes Mountains of Peru.

Medecolin (may day coh leen) were a tribe of evil sorcerers in the myths of Algonquian Native American people.

Medicine (MEHD uh sihn) **man** is a wise man or shaman who has special powers. Medicine men also appear as beings with special powers in myths of Africa and North and South America. Also see **Shaman.**

Midgard (MIHD gahrd) in Norse myths was the world of people.

Muspell (MOOS pehl) in Norse myths was part of the Underworld. It was a place of fire.

N

Nidavellir in Norse myths was the land of the dwarfs.

Niflheim in Norse myths was part of the Underworld. It included Hel, the kingdom of the dead.

Nirvana (nur VAH nuh) in the religion of Buddhism is a state of happiness that people find when they have freed themselves from wanting things. People who reach Nirvana no longer have to be reborn.

O

Oracle (AWRR uh kuhl) in ancient Greece was a sacred place served by people who could foretell the future. Greeks journeyed there to ask questions about their fortunes. Also see **Soothsayer.**

P

Pacariqtambo (pahk kah ree TAHM boh) in Inca myths was a place of three caves from which the first people stepped out into the world. It is also called Paccari Tampu.

Poppykettle was a clay kettle made for brewing poppy-seed tea. In an Inca myth, a poppykettle was used for a boat.

Prophecy (PRAH feh see) is a prediction made by someone who foretells the future.

R

Ragnarok (RAHG nah ruhk) in Norse myths was the final battle of good and evil, in which the giants would fight against the gods of Asgard.

S

Sahara (sah HAH rah) is a vast desert that covers much of northern Africa.

Seriema was a bird in a Carajá myth of South America whose call led the first people to try to find their way from underground to the surface of the earth.

Shaman (SHAH muhn) can be a real person, a medicine man or wise person who knows the secrets of nature. Shamans also appear as beings with special powers in some myths of North and South America. Also see **Medicine man.**

Soothsayer (sooth SAY ur) in ancient Greece was someone who could see into the future. Also see **Oracle.**

Svartalfheim (SVAHRT uhl hym) in Norse myths was the home of the dark elves.

T

Tar Baby was a sticky doll made of tar used to trap Brer Rabbit, a tricky rabbit in African American folk tales.

Tara (TAH rah) in Irish myths was the high seat, or ruling place, of the Irish kings.

Trickster (TRIHK stur) **animals** are clever ones that appear in many myths of North America, South America, and Africa.

Trojan horse. See **Wooden horse of Troy.**

Tuatha dÈ Danann (THOO uh huh day DUH nuhn) were the people of the goddess Danu. Later they were known as gods of Ireland themselves.

V

Vanaheim (VAH nah hym) in Norse myths was the home of the fertility gods.

W

Wadjet eye was a symbol used by the people of ancient Egypt. It stood for the eye of the gods Ra and Horus and was supposed to bring luck.

Wheel of Transmigration (tranz my GRAY shuhn) in the religion of Buddhism is the wheel people's souls reach after they die. From there they are sent back to earth to be born into a higher or lower life.

Wooden horse of Troy was a giant wooden horse built by the Greeks during the Trojan War. The Greeks hid soldiers in the horse's belly and left the horse for the Trojans to find.

Y

Yang (yang) is the male quality of light, sun, heat, and dryness in Chinese beliefs. Yang struggles with Yin for control of things.

Yatkot was a magical tree in an African myth of the Alur people.

Yggdrasil (IHG drah sihl) in Norse myths was a mighty tree that held all three worlds together and reached up into the stars.

Yin (yihn) is the female quality of shadow, moon, cold, and water in Chinese beliefs. Yin struggles with Yang for control of things.

CUMULATIVE INDEX

This is an alphabetical list of important topics covered in all eight volumes of the **World Book Myths and Legends** series. Next to each entry is at least one pair of numbers separated by a slash mark (/). For example, the entry for Argentina is "**Argentina 8/4**". The first number tells you what volume to look in for information. The second number tells you what page you should turn to in that volume. Sometimes a topic appears in more than one place. When it does, additional volume and page numbers are given. Here's a reminder of the volume numbers and titles: 1, *African Myths and Legends*; 2, *Ancient Egyptian Myths and Legends*; 3, *Ancient Greek Myths and Legends*; 4, *Celtic Myths and Legends*; 5, *Chinese Myths and Legends*; 6, *Norse Myths and Legends*; 7, *North American Myths and Legends*; 8, *South American Myths and Legends*.

For information on other World Book products, visit our Web site at www.worldbook.com or call 1-800-WORLDBK (967-5325).

For information on sales to schools and libraries, call 1-800-975-3250.

Cover background illustration by Paul Perreault

World Book, Inc.
233 North Michigan Avenue
Chicago, IL 60601

Pages 1–47: format and illustrations, ©1997 Belitha Press; text, ©1997 Philip Ardagh

Printed in Hong Kong
2 3 4 5 6 7 8 9 10 10 09 08 07 06 05 04 03 02

ISBN(set): 0-7166-2613-6
African Myths and Legends
ISBN: 0-7166-2605-5
LC: 2001026492
Ancient Egyptian Myths and Legends
ISBN: 0-7166-2606-3
LC: 2001026501
Ancient Greek Myths and Legends
ISBN: 0-7166-2607-1
LC: 2001035959
Celtic Myths and Legends
ISBN: 0-7166-2608-X
LC: 20011026496
Chinese Myths and Legends
ISBN: 0-7166-2609-8
LC: 2001026489
Norse Myths and Legends
ISBN: 0-7166-2610-1
LC: 2001026488
North American Myths and Legends
ISBN: 0-7166-2611-X
LC: 2001026490
South American Myths and Legends
ISBN: 0-7166-2612-8
LC: 2001026491